THE LINCOLNSHIRE LANDSCAPE
An Exploration

Jon Fox

ABOVE: **near Worlaby, Lincolnshire Wolds**

First published in 2015 by Green Plover Books
21 Cambridge Avenue, Lincoln, LN1 1LS
www.greenploverbooks.co.uk

Text and photographs by Jon Fox

Copyright © Jon Fox 2015

All rights reserved. No part of this publication may be reproduced, stored in a retrieval system or transmitted in any form or by any means, electronic, mechanical, photocopying or otherwise without prior written permission from the publisher

Dedication: To Lois and to my parents, Alan and Val

ISBN: 978-0-9932696-0-8

Design by Jon Fox. Map artwork by David Would

Printed by L.E.G.O. S.p.A., Vicenza, Italy

RIGHT: winter evening in the Witham Fens

Contents

1. Introduction — 4
2. The Natural Elements — 12
3. The Human Landscape — 28
4. Perceptions — 52
5. The Future — 66

THE LANDSCAPE CHARACTER AREAS:

- I Isle of Axholme — 80
- II Vale of Trent — 92
- III Heath & Cliff — 104
- IV Kesteven Uplands — 120
- V Fens & The Wash — 134
- VI Mid Lindsey Vale — 150
- VII Wolds — 162
- VIII Marsh & Coast — 176

Further Reading — 192

Acknowledgements — 192

1 : Introduction

Lincolnshire lies on the east coast of England between East Anglia and Yorkshire, forming a blunt protrusion of land that stretches as a physical and historic entity from the Wash to the Humber. The long, sandy arc of the North Sea coastline defines Lincolnshire's present terrestrial limit, while inland it reaches to the lower Trent Valley on the west and links with the rolling Jurassic scarplands of central England on the south-west. The southern and north-western boundaries lie almost hidden within England's two largest former wetlands – the Fens and Humberhead Levels respectively – which Lincolnshire shares with adjoining counties.

Thus bounded, Lincolnshire is still something of a land apart, with natural and historic characteristics that have moulded a distinctive landscape and a quiet sense of separateness from surrounding regions that persists today despite modern communications. This is due mainly to its physical distance from major centres of population and its largely rural character. Industry has touched all of the county to some degree, especially Lincoln and the larger towns, and makes a significant contribution to the landscape in the far north around Scunthorpe and the Humber Bank. However, Lincolnshire is still dominated by its vast, rural countryside, which has some of the lowest population densities in lowland England and an unsurpassed feeling of spaciousness.

FACING PAGE: **chalk hills, South Ormsby, Lincolnshire Wolds**

RIGHT: **willows in the Glen Washes, Baston Fen**

Lincolnshire encompasses a wide variety of landscapes and topographies reflecting its large size and diverse geology. Natural habitats range from lowland peat bogs to chalk hills and from sandy heathland to coastal marshes and dunes. This variety is mirrored in the farmed countryside too, which combines with the natural framework to define a number of distinct landscape character areas as described and explored later in this book. Nevertheless, there are generic qualities throughout, including a sweeping topography of open vistas and unbounded skies and a highly intensive approach to agriculture that reflects Lincolnshire's pre-eminence nationally as a producer of food since the mid 19th century. To some

extent these shared physical and cultural aspects have tended to unite Lincolnshire's diverse landscapes into its own, singular landscape identity. Similarities do exist with neighbouring areas, particularly where the natural landscape straddles a historic boundary, such as the Fens, or there is comparable geology, such as the twin chalk uplands of the Lincolnshire Wolds and Yorkshire Wolds. Lincolnshire also displays the broader characteristics of eastern England, including its relatively subdued relief, dry climate, arable dominance in farming and the visual and cultural associations with Denmark and the Low Countries. Nevertheless, Lincolnshire looks and feels different from both East Anglia and Yorkshire and is distinct even as a nominal part of the East Midlands region.

Many writers have emphasised the isolation of Lincolnshire historically, especially prior to the Industrial Revolution and the coming of the railways, suggesting that the "natural barriers" of the Fens, Humber wetlands and River Trent created a near-island that was cut off culturally and economically from surrounding areas. The Anglo-Saxon kingdom of Lindsey, approximating to the northern half of Lincolnshire, has often been portrayed in these terms. Conversely, others have pointed out that the rivers were important routes for migration, settlement and trade. Lincolnshire's Jurassic limestone ridge has also been a natural causeway facilitating movement and integration for millennia, as evidenced by the prehistoric

FACING PAGE: **snow on the Wolds near Normanby-le-Wold**

TOP LEFT: **sandy coast near Mablethorpe**

LEFT: **sunset over the Vale of Trent from Coleby**

'Jurassic Way' and Roman Ermine Street, which still traverses western Lincolnshire from Stamford to the Humber. The reality was therefore probably somewhere between these two perspectives, and mild peripherality rather than isolation best describes the context for Lincolnshire's landscape development and its character today.

The Landscape Character Areas

Various approaches have been used in the past to subdivide Lincolnshire into areas, mostly based on geology directly or on related features such as soils or types of farming. More recently landscape characterisation has developed, using both natural and historic landscape components to define character areas, of which Natural England's National Character Areas are perhaps the best known. The map on page 78 shows the character areas used in this book, which broadly follow the Natural England scheme. It is stressed that the areas are not uniform throughout, nor self-contained; their boundaries were often important for human activity and settlement.

Dutch double? The historic influence of Dutch culture and knowledge can still be traced in Lincolnshire's landscape, including architecture, agriculture and drainage. Dutch gables are occasionally seen on older buildings such as here at **Epworth, Isle of Axholme** (TOP LEFT). Much more widespread are red clay pantiles which were imported from the Netherlands from the 1700s and later manufactured in Lincolnshire, becoming the commonest roofing material until the railways brought in Welsh slate. **Tulip growing in the Fens** (LEFT) has declined drastically since its mid 20th century heyday but many of Lincolnshire's wetland and coastal landscapes resemble the Low Countries. This scene is on the **River Welland at Deeping St. James** (FACING PAGE).

Lincolnshire is divided historically into three Parts – Holland, Kesteven and Lindsey – each with its distinct character and heritage. This, together with the sheer size and diversity of Lincolnshire, challenges the notion of a unified landscape identity across the historic county as a whole. Landscape character is most evident in the individual character areas, each of which has its own personality based on local geology, ecology, built heritage and cultural traditions. Nevertheless, aspects of the landscape and its history play an important part in defining Lincolnshire's overall character and sense of belonging.

FACING PAGE: **ploughland near Burwell, Wolds**

ABOVE: **mud and stud cottage, Ludborough, Lincolnshire Marsh**. Mud and stud is a construction technique indigenous to Lincolnshire and was used across much of the county until the 19th century.

RIGHT: **retired farmer in 2005, Moulton Marsh, Fens**

2 : The Natural Elements

The main elements of nature – earth, air, water and life – have interacted dynamically over millennia to create an evolving natural framework that still underpins Lincolnshire's landscape today.

Earth: rocks & landforms

Lincolnshire has a relatively straightforward though varied geology. The underlying pattern is one of north-south running bands of sedimentary rocks that were laid down in mostly marine environments in the Mesozoic era and subsequently uplifted and tilted with an easterly dip by earth movements in the Tertiary period. The bands of exposed rocks thus become successively younger from west to east, while their differential resistance to erosion has led to the characteristic terrain of alternate uplands and lowlands that defines Lincolnshire's present-day topography.

FACING PAGE: **Trent Cliff near Burton-upon-Stather.** This scarp feature overlooking the River Trent is created by Lower Lias limestones and ironstones and provides extensive views west over the flatlands of the Humberhead Levels. These rock strata mark the beginning of the Jurassic period and the shift from the red desert conditions of the late Triassic to marine conditions.

RIGHT: **Newton Cliff, Newton-on-Trent.** The River Trent has created this unusual exposure of Triassic Mercia Mudstone by eroding steep bluffs of red marl. These rocks are thought to have been deposited as vast mudflats in which the crystallization of salts has left beds of gypsum, as seen protruding here.

LEFT: **Wolds scarp near Tealby.** Even Lincolnshire's hardest rocks rarely form visible outcrops at the surface, but the sandstones of the Lower Cretaceous are an exception. These strata are exposed in the west and south of the Wolds and very occasionally create rocky features as here on the western scarp. Both sandstones and limestones from this rock series have been quarried locally as building stone.

BOTTOM LEFT: **The Lincoln Edge at Coleby.** The resistant Lincolnshire Limestone of the middle Jurassic creates a distinctive scarp or 'cliff' along its western edge where the land rises suddenly above the softer rocks of the Vale of Trent. The Lincoln Edge runs for some 60 miles (97km) from the Leicestershire border near Grantham to the Humber and is a defining feature in the landscape of west Lincolnshire. It is thought to have been a major migration route for prehistoric peoples as part of the 'Jurassic Way' which links through to the Cotswolds and South West England. The spring line at the base of the limestone has attracted settlement along the Lincoln Edge since at least Anglo-Saxon times.

The harder rocks form uplands with steep west-facing scarps and much shallower eastern dip slopes, of which the limestones and ironstones of the Jurassic stone belt and the Cretaceous sandstones and chalk of the Wolds are the main instances. Lower Lias limestones and ironstones form a more subdued series of low hills and scarps just east of the Trent Valley, including the striking Trent Cliff near Burton-upon-Stather. West of the Trent, the Triassic Mercia Mudstone forms another gentle upland, but this lies mainly within Nottinghamshire and dips into Lincolnshire only along the Trent Valley and as the isolated 'islands' of the Isle of Axholme. The softer rocks, mainly clays, form the bedrock of the intervening vales and the Fen basin, eroded down to present-day levels by weathering and glacial action. The coastal Lincolnshire Marsh is clearly a lowland landscape but is anomalous in being based on a sea-cut platform of chalk which has subsequently been covered by glacial and wetland deposits.

Superimposed on this bedrock geology is the much younger 'drift' or Quaternary geology of the last 2 million years, including Ice Age and more recent deposits. Successive glaciations in the Pleistocene (Ice Age) moulded Lincolnshire's landscape through the action of ice sheets which smoothed the uplands and deepened the vales while depositing extensive blankets of pebbly clay called 'till' (formerly known as Boulder Clay). Tills have survived widely, especially in the Lincolnshire Marsh and in parts of the Trent and Mid Lindsey Vales. By contrast, Lincolnshire's uplands are comparatively free of such deposits and have light soils based directly on limestone or chalk, though the Kesteven Uplands are an exception to this pattern. When ice retreated seasonally and during interglacial periods, meltwaters further altered the landscape, creating overflow channels between valleys in the Wolds and leaving deposits along rivers and in outwash plains. It is thought that the wide break in the chalk between the Wolds and Norfolk may have resulted primarily from glacial erosion, thus allowing the creation of the Wash as sea levels rose again.

Also of Pleistocene age are the inland sand deposits called Coversands, of which Lincolnshire has probably the best examples in Britain. These originated by the erosion of the Triassic sandstones west of the River Trent, the reddish grains of which were carried by westerly winds after the final glacial retreat and gradually accumulated to form inland dune systems,

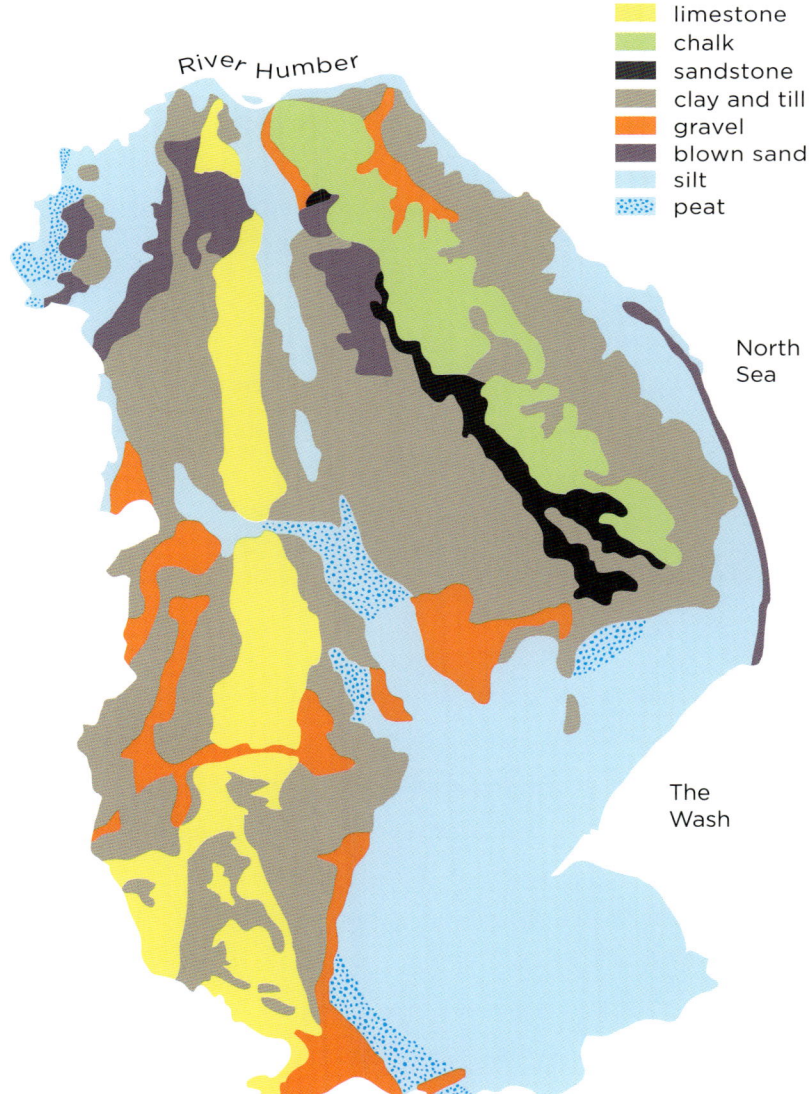

Lincolnshire's geology – the main rock types

especially along river bluffs and scarps. Today, Coversands occur patchily along the Trent Valley between Collingham and Gainsborough and more extensively around Scunthorpe and Market Rasen where they produce their own distinct landscape. For centuries this was sandy heathland maintained by grazing and warrening but sadly most of this habitat has been lost since the 18th century due to the cessation of grazing and other land use changes.

The youngest surfaces are those of the former wetland areas including the Fens, Humberhead Levels and coastal Outmarsh. Deposits here include both silt and peat and reflect complex patterns of wetland evolution

ABOVE: **relict dunes, Risby Warren.** Coversands still occupy extensive tracts across northern Lincolnshire despite loss of sand due to mineral extraction, urban development and reclamation for farmland. In the 20th century many remaining areas were afforested with conifers but fragments of sandy heath vegetation survive in places such as Risby Warren near Scunthorpe, which also has well-preserved dune systems. Where grazing prevents the development of scrub and woodland, the Coversands support a variety of habitats including heather, sand sedge and lichen heaths, acid grassland and even wetland areas. In recent years action to consolidate and recreate heathland on the Coversands in Lincolnshire and Nottinghamshire has been taken by the local wildlife trusts and others.

and reclamation. Wetland creation was driven primarily by rising sea levels after the Ice Age. This caused inundation of the coastal lowlands and shallower river gradients, leading to silting and poor drainage of low-lying areas. Forests that had colonised the lowlands as the climate warmed were slowly drowned and buried, surviving today as the 'bog oaks' of the Fens and the submerged forests of the Lincolnshire coast.

However, sea level fluctuated within this overall rising trend, and a succession of marine advances and retreats caused alternate deposition of marine or tidal silt and freshwater peat, particularly in the Fenland basin. From Medieval times onwards, human intervention progressively stabilised the wetlands through flood defence works and drainage improvements and effectively fixed the coastline at a point in history. Today, marine silts form the land surface around the Wash and in the Outmarsh while alluvial silt dominates the Trent and Ancholme floodplains. Peat is exposed mainly along the inland margin of the Fens and in the remaining peat mires of the Isle of Axholme in the Humberhead Levels.

The wetlands of Lincolnshire are formed from material that is very young in geological terms. In the Lincolnshire Marsh and around the Wash, marine silts were deposited following the Roman period, covering the existing land surface and its archaeology. Silt and clay continue to be deposited in places along the coast, as here in the Wash at **Butterwick Marsh** (TOP RIGHT). Peat developed in freshwater or brackish swamps inland of the coast and, despite ongoing losses from oxidation and erosion, still forms the surface in parts of the Isle of Axholme and Fens. These **'bog oaks'** (RIGHT) have been recovered from fen peat near Bourne and are the remains of ancient trees, mainly Scots pine, killed by the expansion of wetland and peat accumulation, probably during the Neolithic or Bronze Age.

Atmosphere: skies & weather

The earth's atmosphere is the main arena for weather systems and forms a constant element in the human experience of landscape. The idea of the sky as an integral part of landscape aesthetics is well expressed in old Dutch painting, though perhaps less established in the appreciation of the English countryside. Lincolnshire's landscape pushes the idea to the extreme with its sweeping topography of far horizons under vast skies. Lincolnshire now markets itself as a county of big skies and many residents and visitors find inspiration in the scale and beauty of its cloudscapes.

The area best known for its spectacular skies is Fenland – also celebrated for its sunrises and sunsets – but most of Lincolnshire offers excellent opportunities for appreciating the sky and clouds, with relatively low atmospheric pollution and bright coastal light. Despite increasing levels of light pollution as elsewhere, Lincolnshire retains the most extensive tracts of dark night sky in the East Midlands region, focused especially in the Wolds and around the Wash.

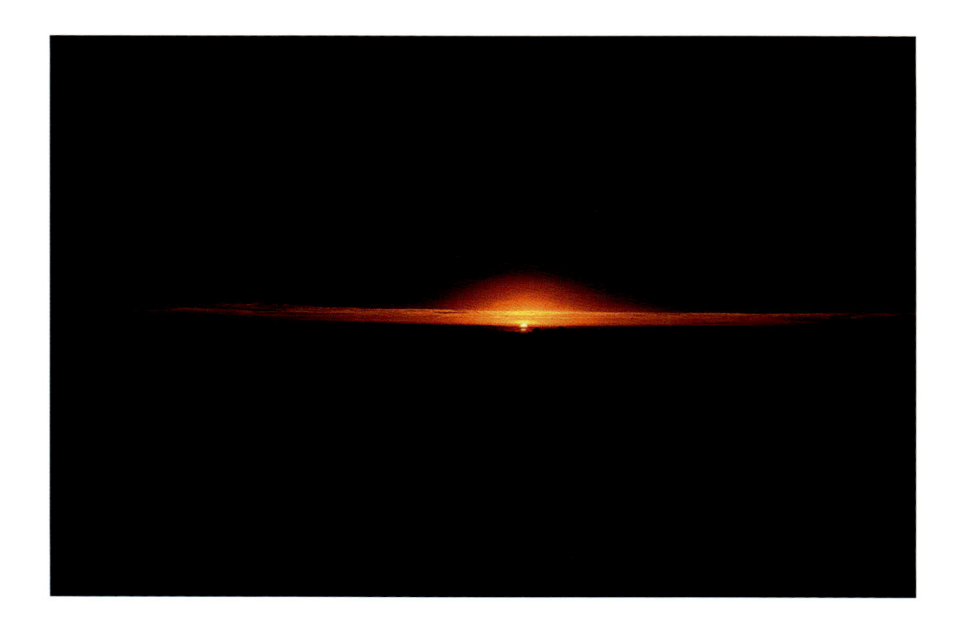

As with the land, however, Lincolnshire's skies almost always display the hand of man. Aircraft contrails are a constant feature and in certain conditions coalesce to form veils of high cloud, while the cooling towers of the Trent Valley power stations generate their own cloud trails. Indeed, the wider impacts of greenhouse gas emissions on climate call into question whether any weather system or cloud formation can be considered to be completely free of human influence in the 21st century.

Climate change is manifested as increasingly erratic weather patterns affecting Lincolnshire, making generalisations about the area's climate much less possible than in the past. Nevertheless, Lincolnshire probably retains for now its overall meteorological character of being sunny and dry relative to the average for England. Other noteworthy facets of 'traditional' Lincolnshire weather are hard winter frosts, cold north-easterlies in spring and above average fogginess.

LEFT: **sunrise from Kirton Drove, Holland Fen**

FACING PAGE: **Marshland sky near Donna Nook**

Foggy Lincolnshire? Lincolnshire has long held a dubious reputation for fog and mist. This is partly the result of early topographic writers who characterised the undrained Fens as a vast malarial swamp. Thomas Dugdale writing in the 1700s, for instance, reiterates an earlier visitor's description of "a hideous fen of huge bigness...ofttimes clouded with moist and dark vapours". Whether this was ever an accurate picture is doubtful and the Fens today are statistically one of the less foggy parts of Lincolnshire. Nevertheless, meteorological records for recent decades place Lincolnshire alongside East Anglia as having more foggy days than most of Central or Southern England though less than the upland areas of the North and West. The Vale of Trent seems particularly prone to morning fog and mist while the coastal fringe of Lincolnshire can experience sea frets in spring and summer that move inland from the North Sea for several miles. Depending on conditions, fogs and frets can be persistent or herald a fine day. When the sun starts to break through, they can create an intimate landscape of obscured distance and strange, ethereal effects that contrasts with Lincolnshire's normally expansive vistas.

TOP LEFT: **mistbow, West Common, Lincoln**

TOP RIGHT: **oak tree and sun in sea fret, Wolds**

Water: rivers, wetlands & the sea

If the atmosphere represents a realm of the imagination and aesthetic appreciation in Lincolnshire, attitudes to liquid water tend to be more practical and utilitarian. Flooding from both the sea and rivers represents a real risk to life and property that has been battled and controlled as far as possible over centuries through drainage and flood defence works.

Lincolnshire's natural drainage pattern has therefore been dramatically modified by the straightening and embanking of rivers and the reclamation of vast tracts of wetland for agriculture and settlement in the Fens, Isle of Axholme and coastal areas. As in the Bedford Level to the south, washlands were created along the main rivers from the 1600s to hold excess floodwaters, while deliberate flooding or 'warping' of land for silt was carried out in the lower Trent Valley in the 18th and 19th centuries to raise the land surface and boost soil fertility.

Water remains a crucial element in the landscape and life of Lincolnshire. Rainfall directly sustains wildlife and crops and also feeds the important aquifers of the area's limestone and chalk formations, thereby supplying

RIGHT: **River Witham at Stapleford, Vale of Trent.** The River Witham follows an unusual arcing course of some 80 miles (130km) from its source in the Leicestershire parish of Wymondham to its outfall in the Wash near Boston. The upper reaches above Grantham have attractive valley scenery while the middle and lower reaches cross the flatlands of the Vale of Trent and Fens respectively and are continuously embanked. The river is navigable from the Wash as far as Brayford Pool in Lincoln.

The majority of Lincolnshire's once vast wetlands have been drained over the centuries for agricultural use, including virtually all of its freshwater fens and carrs. Man-made drainage channels, embanked rivers and washlands are now defining features of the wetland landscape, though these often provide valuable habitats for wildlife as here in the **Witham Fens** (LEFT). Exceptionally, lowland peat bog has survived in the Isle of Axholme, including **Crowle Moors** (BELOW). The latter form part of a larger raised mire complex extending into Yorkshire as Thorne Moors. Peat started to accumulate here between 4,000 and 5,000 years ago when rising sea levels hindered the natural drainage of the Humberhead floodplains. Both this area and the nearby Hatfield Moors were designated as the Humberhead Peatlands National Nature Reserve in 2005 following the cessation of commercial peat extraction.

ABOVE: **chalk stream near Belleau, Wolds**

RIGHT: **River Welland near Tallington**

both natural springs and borehole abstraction of water for household consumption, agriculture and industry. Springs originating from the chalk aquifer have clear, mineral-rich water with a relatively constant temperature that sustains the attractive chalk streams along the eastern margin of the Wolds. The artesian springs known as 'blow wells' near Tetney and elsewhere in the Marsh occur where water escapes under pressure from the chalk aquifer via lenses of sand in the overlying glacial deposits.

The waters of Lincolnshire all drain ultimately into the North Sea via either the Wash or the Humber, both of which are important estuaries ecologically and culturally. Tidal influence on the Rivers Nene, Welland and Witham is controlled by sluices near their outfalls but the River Trent is tidal as far as Cromwell Lock near Newark-on-Trent (Notts) and has its own tidal bore called the aegre or aegir.

Unlike the eroding coastlines of Yorkshire and East Anglia, sheltered parts of Lincolnshire's coast have historically received sediment from the North Sea, especially around the Wash and Humber estuary, where it has created land for reclamation. However, rising sea levels caused by the sinkage of eastern England and global warming are expected to reverse this coastal expansion over the coming decades. The more exposed coastline between Skegness and Mablethorpe is already experiencing increased erosion.

Life: habitats & wildlife

Lincolnshire's varied natural environment is reflected in its diverse wildlife and ecology. Agricultural reclamation and the intensification of farming have left most natural habitats highly fragmented but the surviving areas are a key asset for conservation, providing opportunities for linkage via habitat corridors to support wildlife migration and increase biodiversity.

Important wetland habitats include the peat bogs of the Humberhead Levels, the re-established wet fen on the Glen Washes at Baston Fen and the nature reserves around the Wash, including the RSPB's Frampton Marsh. Increasingly, drainage and flood management practices are encompassing nature conservation as an objective and moving away from the heavily engineered solutions used in the past on Lincolnshire's rivers and coast.

Heathland has fared slightly better than wetland but is also fragmented, occurring mainly on the Coversands and the sandy outwash gravels of the River Bain around Woodhall Spa. Careful management is required to prevent heathland reverting to scrub and woodland, with grazing by sheep or cattle often used as a modern alternative to burning.

TOP RIGHT: **Common heather in bloom, Kirkby Moor**

RIGHT: **Field mouse-ear growing on Coversands, Risby Warren**

FACING PAGE: **Brent geese in winter, Frampton Marsh**

Despite being one of the UK's least wooded counties in percentage terms Lincolnshire is rich in semi-natural woodland, with the clay areas of the vales and Kesteven Uplands having particular concentrations. Lincolnshire's limewoods are of national importance, the main focus being the Bardney Limewoods National Nature Reserve near Wragby. Forestry plantations are another significant contributor to woodland in Lincolnshire, with the Coversands providing the largest area.

Lincolnshire has rich coastal habitats, including dune systems, salt marsh and mudflats, and both the Wash and the Humber estuary are of international importance for birds. The Wash is arguably Lincolnshire's greatest natural feature, combining spectacular wildlife and a vast landscape of real wildness. However, exploration of its marshes and sandbanks can be dangerous without a detailed knowledge of local geography and tides.

Grasslands are the habitat that has seen the greatest loss since World War II, with the shift to arable farming dramatically reducing all categories including pasture, meadow and chalk grassland. Most surviving fragments with high ecological value are now managed as nature reserves, though wider areas of traditional grazing land in the Lincolnshire Marsh are also being targeted for conservation-based farming.

Farmland makes up the greater proportion of the rural landscape and is an important wildlife resource in its own right. Much remains to be done to

LEFT: **spring flowers in Chambers Farm Wood, Bardney Limewoods**

RIGHT: **chalk grassland near Rothwell, Wolds**

BOTTOM RIGHT: **arable field with poppies, Brattleby Cliff**

reverse the ecological damage that intensive farming has caused, but farmland in Lincolnshire is seldom the wildlife desert that is sometimes portrayed in the media. In recent years a shift to more wildlife-friendly farming practices, including hedge and tree planting and the use of conservation and game strips around fields, has started to boost the biodiversity of the countryside. Both marsh harrier and Montagu's harrier are now breeding again in the Lincolnshire Fens and the wider countryside continues to support populations of farmland species including skylark, corn bunting, yellowhammer, whitethroat, lesser whitethroat, lapwing, partridge and brown hare.

3 : The Human Landscape

Man has interacted with Lincolnshire's natural framework over millennia to produce the landscape we see today. Perhaps more intensely than any other part of England it is a landscape created and maintained by farming. Successive waves of change in agriculture and its social organisation have moulded the countryside and left a legacy that can be traced in land use, field patterns and settlement. Today, Lincolnshire's landscape is dominated by intensive arable farming yet still retains features and archaeology from every period of man's use of the environment. This chapter looks at the main human developments that have made the landscape, focusing primarily on agriculture and settlement but also touching on other aspects such as industry, religion and defence.

The landscape before farming: Ice Ages and early man

The story of humans in the Lincolnshire landscape is thought to begin with the occupation of Britain by early hominids during the Cromerian interglacial period between 700,000 and 450,000 years ago. At this time

FACING PAGE: **ruined church and village site, Calceby, Wolds**. Calceby is one of around 235 Deserted Medieval Villages in Lincolnshire. The village's population declined slowly after the 13th century due probably to one or more factors including the end of feudalism, a shift to sheep farming and famine. The ruined church is the most obvious survival today and the Medieval streets, house foundations and fields are visible only as markings in the surrounding pasture.

Britain was joined to mainland Europe via an extensive plain covering the North Sea basin, sometimes termed Doggerland, with the area that later became Lincolnshire occupying an inland position. Along with east-flowing river systems that were the precursors of the modern Trent, Witham and Humber, a major river called the Bytham River flowed from the West Midlands to East Anglia and beyond, cutting a gap through the Jurassic limestone in south Lincolnshire near Castle Bytham. Little is known about these earliest hunter-gatherer people but archaeological finds in the Bytham River valley indicate that it may have been an important regional route for movement and colonization in Britain.

The subsequent Anglian glaciation (450,000 to 375,000 years ago) ended this first human occupation of Lincolnshire as well as transforming the pre-Anglian landscape. The Bytham River was obliterated and its limestone gap filled by glacial till. Re-occupation by man between the Anglian and the final or Devensian glaciation (70,000 to 10,000 years ago) is very sparsely evidenced in Lincolnshire by finds of early stone hand axes in river gravel deposits near Lincoln and flints on higher ground in the Wolds at Salmonby and Kirmington. This period encompassed both warm and cold stages, with corresponding fluctuations in sea level that successively exposed and flooded Doggerland. The warm interglacial peak of around 125,000 years ago saw species such as hippopotamus in Lincolnshire and a coastline of high chalk cliffs along the eastern side of the Wolds, though humans do not appear to have been present in Britain at this time.

The Devensian glaciation probably prevented human occupation over much of Britain in its coldest phases but nevertheless saw the arrival of Neanderthal and then Modern man. Speculatively, mobile bands of hunter-gatherers ranged across open grassland or tundra environments including the Lincolnshire area, possibly from nearby cave settlements such as Cresswell Crags (Derbys/Notts), if not actually settling here.

Lincolnshire emerged from the Devensian glaciation with a natural topography of uplands and vales more akin to the present pattern, though it still extended eastward into Doggerland until rising sea levels finally separated Britain as an island around 7,000 years ago. As the glaciers retreated and the meltwater lakes drained away, an open landscape was followed by forest recolonisation, initially birch, pine and hazel, then temperate species including oak, ash, lime and elm. The archaeological remains of Mesolithic hunter-gathering in Lincolnshire are dominated by 'microlith' tools and indicate a move to smaller hunting territories as the period progressed, with settlement occurring in favourable environments such as Risby Warren. Other evidence such as pollen analysis suggests that human manipulation of the environment probably began at this time with forest clearance to encourage game animals.

Early Agriculture: Neolithic to Anglo-Saxon

The introduction of agriculture into Lincolnshire occurred in the Neolithic period, probably before 4,000 BC, with mobile communities of livestock herders superseding the old hunter-gatherer lifestyle. Opinions differ on how densely wooded Britain was at this time, but evidence from the Kesteven Uplands suggests widespread management of the landscape through felling and burning, with 'slash and burn' settlement in favourable locations such as river valleys and fen edges, and the creation of savannah-like expanses of heath and woodland for hunting on the uplands. Further systematic clearance of woodland for farming occurred in Kesteven in the early Bronze Age around 2,500 to 2,100 BC, as evidenced by clay sediment washed into the Fen basin.

LEFT: **Waddington Heath under snow**

FACING PAGE: **heathland in the Trent Valley**. Prehistoric finds in Lincolnshire suggest that the light soils such as the Coversands and river gravels were favoured locations for Mesolithic and Neolithic settlements. Early agriculture here is thought to have contributed to the creation of heathland through soil exhaustion and leaching.

The Bronze Age also saw the introduction of more permanent settlements and the first fields. One of the best-known sites nationally is located at Fengate near Peterborough (Cambs), but the remains of comparable settlements with field systems have also been found in Lincolnshire along the Welland valley and Fen edge in Kesteven. These sites indicate Bronze Age communities using fenland as summer grazing for livestock, with arable cropping and winter pasture on the adjoining uplands. A similar pattern was probably repeated further north along the wetland edges of the Heath, Cliff and Lincolnshire Wolds.

Despite cooler conditions and encroaching wetlands, the Iron Age saw agriculture expand across much of Lincolnshire. By the time of the Roman invasion, Lincolnshire had probably already attained its relatively thinly wooded character and a prosperous agricultural landscape dominated by scattered farming settlements within extensive field systems. Archaeology is revealing a high degree of continuity from the original laying out of fields and settlements in the Iron Age (or even earlier) through the Romano-British and early Anglo-Saxon periods, albeit that farming regimes and technologies evolved and changed. Romano-British agriculture emphasised grain production to feed the Roman army and generate an economic surplus. Arable was focused in the uplands and vales, where most villas were also located, and not in the Fens as once thought. The Roman Fenland was mainly used for rearing cattle and salt production.

The Romano-British period is the first for which obvious remains of farming have survived in the present-day landscape, in the form of stepped cultivation terraces. These can be seen in several places in the

ABOVE: **Fiskerton Fen, near Lincoln.** This round building is a modern bird hide inspired by an Iron Age dwelling. The fens of the Witham valley below Lincoln have yielded important Bronze Age and Iron Age finds including wooden canoes, timber causeways and spectacular metalwork including the famous Witham Shield, now in the British Museum. The archaeology of the area indicates that various materials were placed in the River Witham as ritual offerings from the Bronze Age until the 14th century, suggesting that pagan practices became Christianised and linked to the numerous monastic sites that emerged along the valley in the Medieval period.

ABOVE: **Gaumer Hill, Lincolnshire Wolds.** This detached hill or 'outlier' of chalk adjoins the chalk scarp line near Scamblesby. The northern flanks have terraced earthworks resembling the strip lynchets of southern and western England. Their original date is uncertain but they could have been constructed in the Romano-British period and are thought to have been used for arable cultivation or vine growing. Similar cultivation terraces can be seen elsewhere in the Wolds at Rowgate Hill and Kirmond-le-Mire.

Lincolnshire Wolds. However, other less obvious landscape features, including early field systems, survive as crop marks that can be detected from the air. In Lincolnshire, these indicate a remarkably high density of settlement during the Iron Age and offer tantalizing clues about the farmed landscapes of the period. For example, linear earthworks crossing the limestone plateau north and south of Lincoln may represent territorial boundaries for managing upland grazing or, alternatively, be banked droveways for moving cattle across the area without damage to crops.

Remaking the countryside (I): villages & open fields

The expansion of agriculture had already established a heavily farmed countryside across much of Lincolnshire by the Iron Age, but the subsequent shift to the open field system during the Anglo-Saxon and Danish periods represented a further massive remodelling of the rural landscape. Away from the Fens, Lincolnshire broadly follows the pattern seen in the Midlands, in which scattered rural settlements and individually farmed fields were superseded by focused or 'nucleated' villages and communal farming under manorial control. Each village was surrounded by its common arable fields (usually two or three in number) plus other land resources including meadow, grazing land and woodland.

The origin of open field farming is debated by landscape historians, but was probably a response to the unpredictable climate and difficult clay soils of the Midland zone, facilitating the rapid deployment of large plough teams when suitable weather arrived. Except in the Fens and Marsh,

ABOVE RIGHT: **open field strips near Haxey, Isle of Axholme.** Open fields and strip farming have survived in the Isle of Axholme to an extent unparalleled anywhere else in England, giving a farmed landscape that is strongly redolent of the Medieval period.

RIGHT: **church and manor house, Bassingthorpe, Kesteven Uplands.** Despite later developments, Lincolnshire's uplands and vales retain their Medieval settlement pattern of nucleated villages each centred on a parish church. This pattern is typical of a central zone of England that runs from Hampshire to Northumberland. The place name element 'thorpe' is common throughout Lincolnshire and like '-by', 'toft' and 'holme' is thought to signify establishment or takeover by Danish settlers.

almost all of Lincolnshire's present-day villages emerged via this process some time between the 8th and 11th centuries and were therefore already in existence by the Domesday Survey of 1086. Open fields would have dominated over large areas by this time, presenting an arable landscape that in places probably rivalled the largest modern 'grain prairies' in its expansiveness, though not wholly without trees or hedges and broken by a ramifying network of meadow and pasture along the rivers and streams.

The Medieval countryside was, however, far from being cultivated throughout. Most of the upland plateau of the Heath, Cliff and Wolds formed a 'heath' of open grassland that was used primarily for grazing livestock and rabbit warrening, while large parts of the wetlands were seasonally flooded and only suitable as summer grazing. Smaller tracts of sandy heathland were also scattered across Lincolnshire, especially on the leached soils of the Coversands and other sands and gravels.

Additionally, from Anglo-Saxon times onwards, defined areas were set aside by the monarch and the aristocracy for hunting and/or rearing deer. Royal hunting areas were termed Forests (not necessarily wooded throughout but subject to so-called Forest Law) of which Kesteven Forest is the main location recorded in Lincolnshire. This was centred on Bourne and encompassed areas of wild fen as well as woodland on the Kesteven

RIGHT: **Grimsthorpe Park.** The park of Grimsthorpe Castle has a complex history involving alterations and additions over several centuries after its initial laying out in the 17th century. However, the original design incorporated elements of an earlier Medieval landscape of ancient pollarded oaks and wood pasture that can still be traced today.

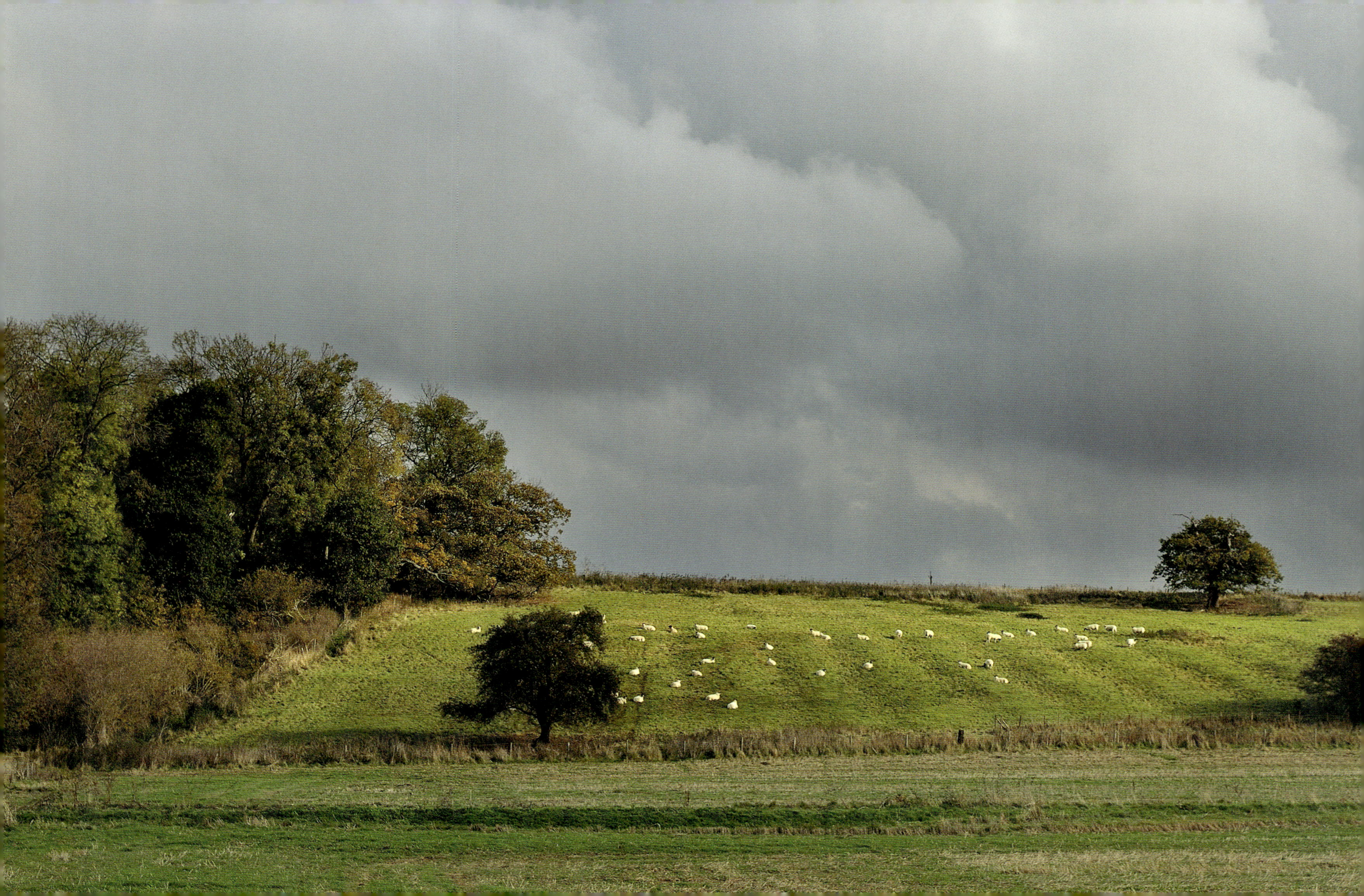

Uplands, though relatively little is known of its history. Far more numerous were deer parks, which were usually privately owned by a lord and would have been fenced areas containing woodland and wood-pasture. Deer parks were distributed widely throughout Lincolnshire outside of the wetland areas. Most declined after the 14th century due to agricultural conversion and other factors but some have left physical and ecological traces in the landscape, especially where they were incorporated into the landscaped parks of country houses.

Prior to the Reformation, monasteries, abbeys and similar religious establishments exerted a major influence on the landscape as landowners with involvement in agriculture, drainage and other activities. Monastic farms called 'granges' were established in many parts of the Lincolnshire countryside in Medieval times and later often became secular estates.

Remaking the countryside (II): Enclosure & the Agricultural Revolution

The privatisation of the open fields and commons to create individual farms was the next great agricultural and social change moulding the Lincolnshire countryside – a process known as enclosure. This brought the progressive replacement of the open field landscape with hedged or walled fields, firstly through privately organised enclosure between the 14th and 18th centuries and then by the Parliamentary enclosures of the late 18th and early 19th centuries. Private or early enclosure usually involved a shift to pastoral farming and was more prevalent in areas of clay soil that supported rich pasture, such as in the vales and Kesteven Uplands. In some places

FACING PAGE: **near Irnham, Kesteven Uplands**. This hillside pasture in the Glen valley shows 'ridge and furrow' markings from earlier strip cultivation. Conversion to grass probably occurred in later Medieval times as the common arable fields gave way to sheep and cattle farming in the changing social and economic conditions that followed the Black Death. Irnham was fully enclosed before the Parliamentary enclosures.

ABOVE: **Slack's Hill, Eagle Hall**. On first sight this scene in the Vale of Trent appears to be a classic example of Parliamentary enclosure with its neat hedged fields and post-Medieval farmstead located away from the village. The area was, however, part of the extra-parochial estate of Eagle Hall established by the Knights Templar and was probably enclosed early. Map evidence suggests that the farmstead is a 19th century addition to an already enclosed landscape, at which time further fields were added by partial clearance of Eagle Hall Farm Wood.

it involved a wholesale shift to sheep farming and may have contributed to the shrinkage and loss of Medieval villages as seen in parts of the Midlands. Field patterns dating from early enclosure are often still identifiable despite subsequent changes, being typically more piecemeal and less regular than those of the Parliamentary enclosures.

Except in parts of the Isle of Axholme, Parliamentary enclosure finally swept away the remaining open field landscape in a tidal wave between 1760 and 1840. Whole parishes were re-ordered, with the village arable and pasture being allocated between the larger landowners in the form of private fields, and all but the least fertile commons and heaths also reclaimed and enclosed for agriculture. Completing this drastic transformation of the countryside were new farmsteads built away from the villages and straight new roads that were sufficiently wide for verges. Parliamentary enclosure

TOP LEFT & LEFT: **Lincoln Heath**. The limestone plateau of the Lincoln Heath was reclaimed for agriculture in the second half of the 18th century during the Parliamentary enclosures and became an exemplar of the new 'corn and sheep' farming. By the mid 19th century, large flocks of Lincoln Longwools were being folded in fields of turnips and other fodder crops to enrich soil fertility as part of new crop rotations that typically also included barley, clover and wheat courses. Many features of the Heath landscape date to the enclosure period, including drystone walls, hedgerows, farmsteads, plantation woods and roads.

FACING PAGE: **Lincoln Longwools near Risby.** After centuries of longwool production in Lincolnshire, the Lincoln Longwool sheep is today maintained largely by rare breed enthusiasts.

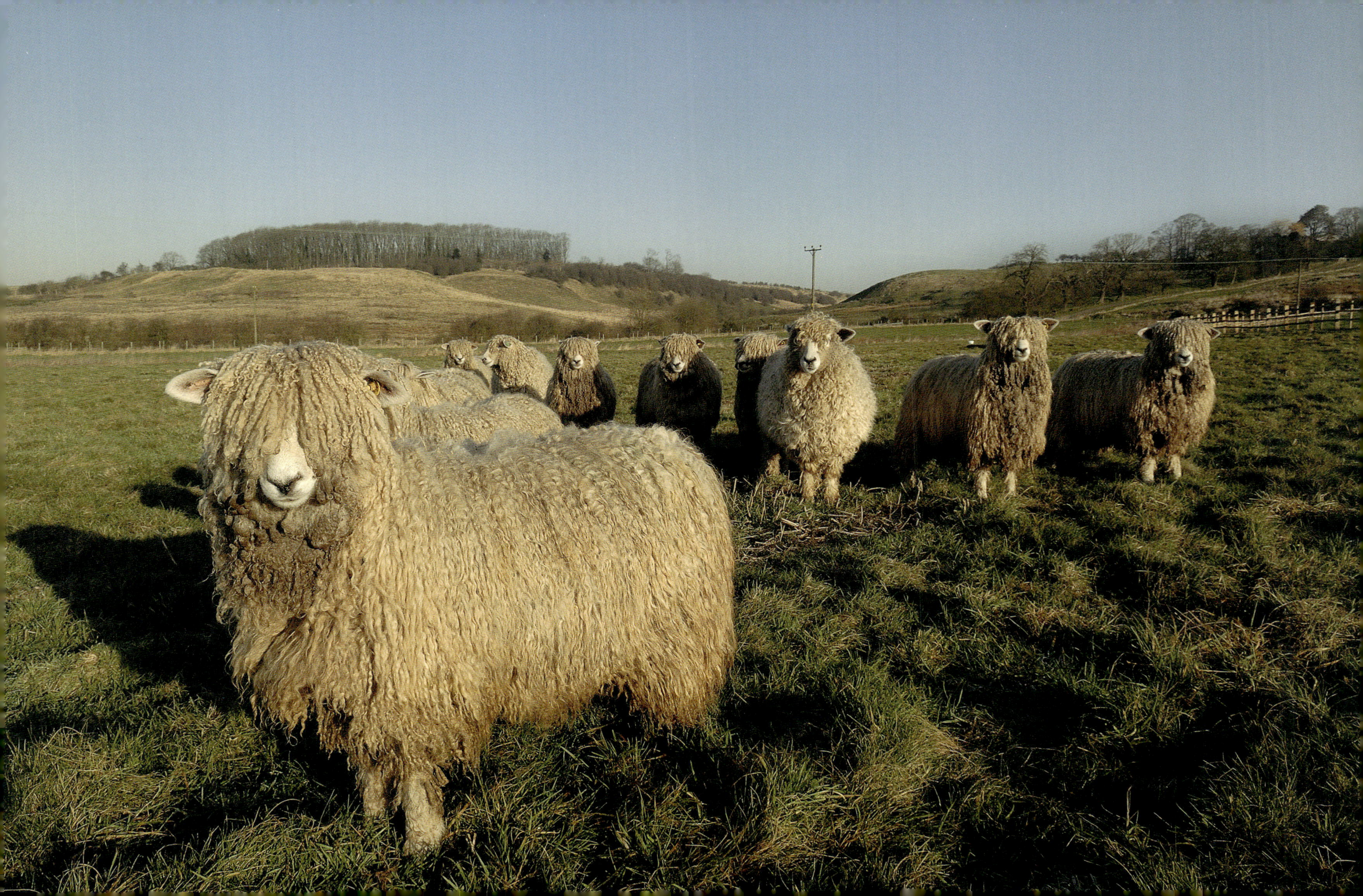

marked the beginning of the Agricultural Revolution in Lincolnshire, facilitating the shift to a more intensive, mixed farming based on new crop rotations, improved breeds of livestock, new techniques for improving soils and even model designs for farm buildings. By the 1850s Lincolnshire was a national leader in this progressive approach to farming – called High Farming – which supplied the rapidly growing population of industrial England with cereals, meat and wool. Lincolnshire's uplands in particular had been transformed from unenclosed sheepwalks and warrens into highly productive 'corn and sheep' farms.

Today, despite subsequent rationalisation, the countryside of the vales and uplands is still based on the patterns established by enclosure. Most fields, and their hedgerows, walls and trees, date back to the enclosure of the open fields and commons, while the restricted public access to land remains as a profound social and political legacy.

As elsewhere in England, the evolving aesthetic and sporting interests of the land-owning class continued to mould the post-Medieval landscape through the development of country house estates, including woodland planting to provide cover for foxes and game. The large estates of Brocklesby in the Wolds and Grimsthorpe in Kesteven are exceptional in the scale and grandeur of their planning, but smaller estates have had a major influence on the landscape across Lincolnshire apart from the wetlands.

TOP LEFT: **Culverthorpe Hall near Sleaford**

LEFT: **avenue of beech trees on the Burton Hall estate, Lincoln Cliff**

The Wetlands: Settlement & Drainage

The history of Lincolnshire's wetlands has always been closely connected to that of its uplands, with the former providing resources – grazing, fish, wildfowl, reed, osier and peat – and therefore attracting people to their margins. Nevertheless, the wetlands also have their own internal landscapes which developed differently from the uplands and vales and which reflect their individual histories of land use, settlement and culture. The landscape of each of the main wetlands is explored more fully in the individual area chapters, but some key features are noted here.

Prior to drainage by man, wetlands occupied approximately one third of Lincolnshire, the main areas being the Fens, the Isle of Axholme and the Lincolnshire Marsh. The term 'wetland' is a convenient label for these low-lying areas but requires care, as only some of the land was permanently wet or inundated even during the wettest periods of history. Before human intervention to control drainage, there was already land that was only wet

ABOVE: **Skidbrooke church, Lincolnshire Marsh**

or flooded seasonally, as well as natural 'islands' and other relatively dry areas suitable for habitation. Nevertheless, variation in the wetness of land and efforts in drainage and flood prevention have fundamentally shaped settlement and land use patterns across the wetland areas.

Medieval settlement in the wetlands typically shows less nucleation than elsewhere in Lincolnshire, with greater dispersal along dykes and droves and the establishment of 'daughter' settlements as land was reclaimed from coastal marshes and inland fens. The classic case is the Fenland, where such expansion occurred from an arc of Anglo-Saxon and Danish settlement on the silt fringe around the Wash known as the Townlands. In the Lincolnshire

Lincolnshire's reclaimed wetlands often retain place names based on their historic origin, which is of two main types. 'Marsh' refers to land reclaimed by the embanking and draining of tidal marshland, while 'fen' (or 'carr' in north Lincolnshire) refers to freshwater wetland reclaimed inland on peat or silt.

TOP RIGHT: **reclaimed marshland, Benington Sea End**

BOTTOM RIGHT: **reclaimed fenland, Northorpe Fen**

FACING PAGE: **Sea Bank, Frampton Marsh**. Earthen banks have been constructed to protect and reclaim land in Lincolnshire's wetlands from at least Anglo-Saxon times. Although named Roman Bank by antiquarians in the 17th century this section of former sea bank at Frampton is now thought to date from the 9th or 10th century. By 1300 the Sea Bank formed a continuous, consolidated sea defence that extended right round the Wash coastline, dividing tidal salt marsh from the farmland and settlements of the Lincolnshire Townlands and Norfolk Marshland. Today the Sea Bank often lies several miles inland of the present coastline.

43

LEFT: **Quadring church, Fens.** Quadring is one of a string of Anglo-Saxon settlements that developed on the low silt ridge around the Wash. The main village is thought to have shifted to its current location during the Black Death, leaving the Medieval church isolated. The daughter hamlet of Quadring Eaudyke adjoins Bicker Haven, a former inlet of the sea that silted up in the Medieval period before being drained and enclosed in the 16th century. Bicker Haven was the estuary of the Witham until 1017 when massive floods diverted the river northwards, thus enabling the port of Boston to develop.

BOTTOM LEFT: **'dylands' preserved in a pasture near Donington, Fens**. This system of broad, flat ridges separated by ditches was probably for improving field drainage and is thought to have been widely used in the reclaimed siltlands of the Lincolnshire Fens from Medieval times. Most dylands have been destroyed by ploughing over the last two centuries as the siltlands of the Fens shifted from the rich pasture of Tudor and Stuart times to intensive arable production. The ditches become flooded after wet weather, as seen here.

Marsh, daughter settlements were established in the Outmarsh for salt making and farming from around the time of the Domesday survey and were responsible for the reclamation of the coastal marshland.

Medieval field systems and the history of enclosure in Lincolnshire's wetlands also differed from the uplands and vales. In the Townlands the main settlements had some arable land farmed in common, but this was typically intermixed with that of free tenants in complex arrangements and became fully privatised well before the Parliamentary enclosures. Additionally, instead of conventional open fields containing furlongs of strips, the Medieval field pattern typically consisted of blocks of narrow, elongated fields surrounded by drainage ditches and often subdivided into strips called 'dylands' or 'dylings'. The latter have only survived agricultural change in a handful of sites but the underlying pattern of fields has often persisted in simplified form. A similar field pattern developed in the coastal siltlands of the Outmarsh, though conventional ridge and furrow strips produced by ploughing are usual here.

In the Isle of Axholme there was little wetland reclamation before the 17th century and the Medieval settlements and common fields were developed on islands of dry land. As noted above, however, the open fields avoided enclosure despite the drainage and enclosure of the surrounding wetlands.

Drainage has played a critical part in producing Lincolnshire's landscape, above all in the wetlands. Mostly it is a story of the rich and powerful forcing their interests over those of wetland communities, who resisted the changes with all possible means including sabotage. Vermuyden's drainage schemes and the violent opposition they met in the Isle of Axholme and Bedford Level are well-known, but similar bitter conflicts occurred across the Lincolnshire Fens in the 17th and 18th centuries. Ultimately the drainers prevailed and private farmland replaced the traditional, communal use of the wetlands that had developed over the preceding centuries.

RIGHT: **Crowle Moors, Isle of Axholme**

Industry in the Landscape

Lincolnshire has never been industrial when compared with neighbours such as Nottinghamshire and Yorkshire and has no legacy of coal mining or large-scale textile manufacturing. However, industry has contributed to its landscape throughout history and even prehistory.

Lincolnshire's low-lying coast of salt marshes and creeks made it a major centre for salt making as early as the Bronze Age. Remains of Bronze Age salterns (salt making sites) occur in locations which are now far inland along the Fen edges and the inland fringe of the Lincolnshire Outmarsh. Peat was probably the fuel used to boil the brine in ceramic pots which survive archaeologically as 'briquetage' fragments. The expansion of peat fen in the Iron Age and Romano-British period pushed salt making nearer to the present coastline, leaving numerous remains in the Fens and around Hogsthorpe in the Marsh. However, most early salterns now lie buried by marine silts or other deposits and rarely impact on the modern landscape.

Salt making was rekindled in Lincolnshire in the Anglo-Saxon period and continued until the 17th century, when it became uncompetitive with other British and Continental producers. Unlike their antecedents, Medieval salterns used filtration to extract brine from coastal sand and silt and produced large amounts of waste material that was deposited in mounds. Saltern debris is still visible in the landscape today, especially around the Wash and in the Outmarsh, where it adds strange undulations to the otherwise flat silt surface. Salt making was an important part of the Medieval economy of the Lincolnshire coast and contributed to the prosperity of both the Townlands and Lincolnshire Marsh. There is clear evidence that many villages in the Outmarsh were established as seasonal daughter settlements primarily for salt production and grazing, and that saltern mounds helped to consolidate the reclamation of coastal marshland by raising the land surface for permanent settlement and farming.

Ironstone is found along the western edges of both the Jurassic uplands and the Lincolnshire Wolds and has been mined and quarried in several locations. Early extraction in Roman and Medieval times is recorded but production began in earnest in the mid 19th century. In particular, the development of large-scale opencast quarrying of the Frodingham ironstone around Scunthorpe and the surrounding villages led to a new industrial town dominated by blast furnaces and steel mills. Production elsewhere in Lincolnshire was mainly in a rural context, including mines

FACING PAGE: **Sibsey Trader Mill, Sibsey, Fens**. This fine tower mill was built in 1877 and is one of the few Lincolnshire windmills in working order today. It is now used to produce organic flour as well as being a visitor attraction. Lincolnshire had hundreds of such windmills in the 19th and early 20th centuries, of which over a hundred survive today in whole or part. Wind power also played an important role in fen drainage before steam pumping. In 1815, there were some 50 windpumps operating in Deeping Fen alone, though these had all gone by about 1850. Sadly, there is no surviving example of this drainage technology anywhere in Lincolnshire today, and the only extant windpump in the Fens is at Wicken Fen (Cambs).

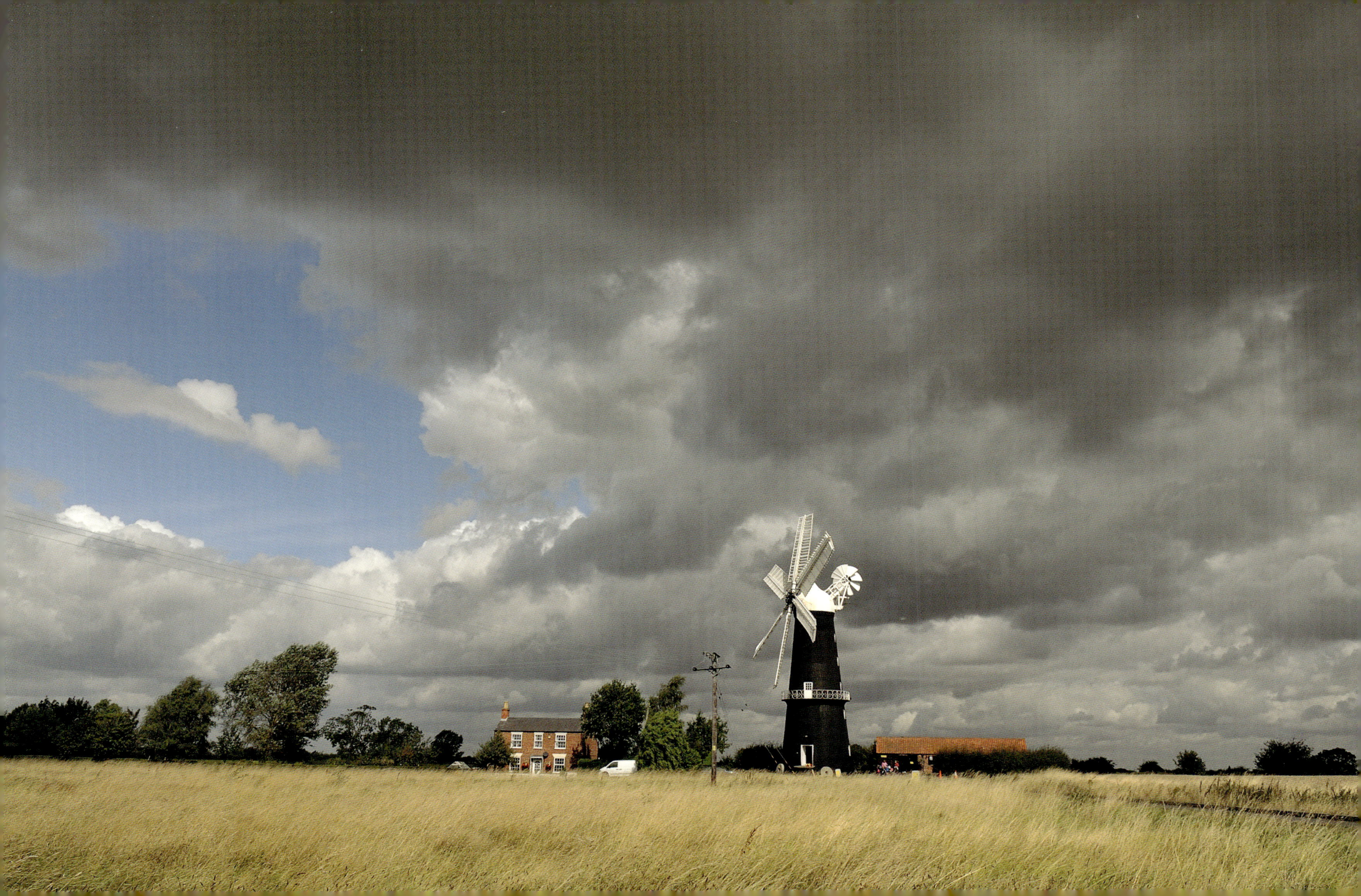

near Nettleton and Claxby in the Wolds and quarrying along the Lincoln Edge from Lincoln to Grantham and beyond. The opencast quarrying around Colsterworth and South Witham commenced in the 1890s with the opening of the railway between Bourne and Saxby (Leics) and continued until the 1970s, leaving a rather forlorn landscape of quarry gulches and restored farmland that extends onto the adjoining limestone plateau of Leicestershire and Rutland.

Other industries that have left significant though localised marks on the Lincolnshire countryside include milling, food processing, quarrying of limestone and chalk, brick and tile making and gravel extraction. Apart from the Scunthorpe area, however, Lincolnshire's only other strongly industrial landscape today lies along the Humber Bank between Grimsby and Killingholme, which forms a near continuous stretch of docks, storage complexes and petrochemical works.

ABOVE: **Scunthorpe Steelworks from Risby Warren**

Landscapes of Spirituality

Evidence for spiritual activity in the British landscape begins with the monuments of the Neolithic, though some archaeologists believe that ritual burial goes back at least to the Mesolithic and probably utilized natural features such as caves. Alongside the development of farming settlements and field systems, Neolithic and Bronze Age society created increasingly complex ritual landscapes with a variety of monuments including barrows, cairns and cursuses, culminating in the circular henges and stone circles of the late Neolithic and early Bronze Age. Such monuments probably represent focal points or 'gateways' within wider ritual landscapes that were set aside as the realm of the ancestors or deities. In Lincolnshire, known Neolithic and Bronze Age barrows and other monuments are concentrated on the Wolds, usually occupying prominent locations on hilltops or rises, though they also occur in other areas. Also of Neolithic origin is the henge at West Ashby near Horncastle.

The Iron Age saw a cultural change from monuments to the ritual placing of objects in places of spiritual significance within the landscape, especially rivers and wetlands. Important finds from such practices in Lincolnshire include those from the Witham valley near Lincoln. There is evidence of continuity of ritual use at the Witham valley sites right into the Medieval period, and the existence of Bronze Age barrow cemeteries in the same vicinity may indicate continuity of significance from earlier times too. Landscape features such as prominent hills and woods were probably also

RIGHT: **St. Andrew's Parish Church, Denton**

important spiritually at least until the start of Christianity, providing suitable places for gathering and/or sacred rituals.

Medieval church building commenced following the re-introduction of Christianity in the Anglo-Saxon period, initially creating 'minster' churches such as Lincoln and Stow that served a wide area. Parish churches emerged in the 10th and 11th centuries in parallel with village nucleation, while monastic houses also became numerous and contributed greatly to Lincolnshire's agricultural and economic development up to the Tudor Reformation. Again, churches and monasteries were sometimes located on or near sites that had previously held sacred significance, such as springs or fen islands, continuing the link between landscape and spirituality. Lincolnshire's parish churches remain as an architectural legacy that is unsurpassed in England though relatively few of its monastic buildings are still upstanding. Nonconformist chapels are common in Lincolnshire's villages, often now converted for residential or other uses.

Today, many people believe that a spiritual connection with the landscape has been lost or eroded. However, the growing use of the countryside for recreation probably represents the latest manifestation of a human need to commune with nature through landscape.

20th Century to Present: Change & Conflict

The 20th century was one of great change in all aspects of the Lincolnshire countryside, not least in farming. The decades following World War II saw a new agricultural revolution based on mechanisation, intensification and the increasing application of science. This resulted in a fundamental shift from 'traditional' mixed farming to arable, with associated landscape changes such as hedgerow removal, field amalgamation and the widespread loss of ancient woodland and other wildlife habitats. The negative ecological impacts of these changes led to a growing acceptance of the need for wildlife and landscape conservation within farming from the 1980s, but the appearance of the Lincolnshire countryside today still strongly reflects this historic transformation from the age of the horse and human labour to the technological age of the tractor, combine harvester and crop sprayer.

Lincolnshire is still widely regarded as the spiritual home of the RAF due to its history of military flight in the last century. Its topography of upland plateaux and location close to the east coast made it ideal for military air bases in both World Wars and subsequently in the Cold War. This has left an important military and defence archaeology as well as sites that are active as bases today. Many former airfields have been returned to agricultural use but the remains of runways, radar stations and other features have survived, along with historic military aircraft including the Battle of Britain Memorial Flight at RAF Coningsby. Today, aviation heritage is a significant and growing element of Lincolnshire's tourism.

Other major changes affecting the landscape over the last century include electricity generation and transmission, urban and rural settlement growth, coastal holiday development, state forestry, telecommunications and the massive growth of traffic and roads. Some of these are now managed through the town and country planning system, which was introduced in 1947 to control the development of land in the public interest.

ABOVE & RIGHT: **former RAF Ingham, Lincoln Cliff.** This disused bomber airfield was created in World War II and was one of 21 such sites in Lincolnshire by April 1945. The airfield was open for just 6 years from 1942 to 1948 and was home to Polish squadrons and the Polish Record Office. Little remains today apart from the decaying concrete runway which is slowly being reclaimed by nature and developing its own ecology.

TOP LEFT: **landing lights for RAF Scampton, Lincoln Cliff.** RAF Scampton is famous as the airfield from which the 1943 Dambuster raids were flown and as the home of the Red Arrows aerial display team.

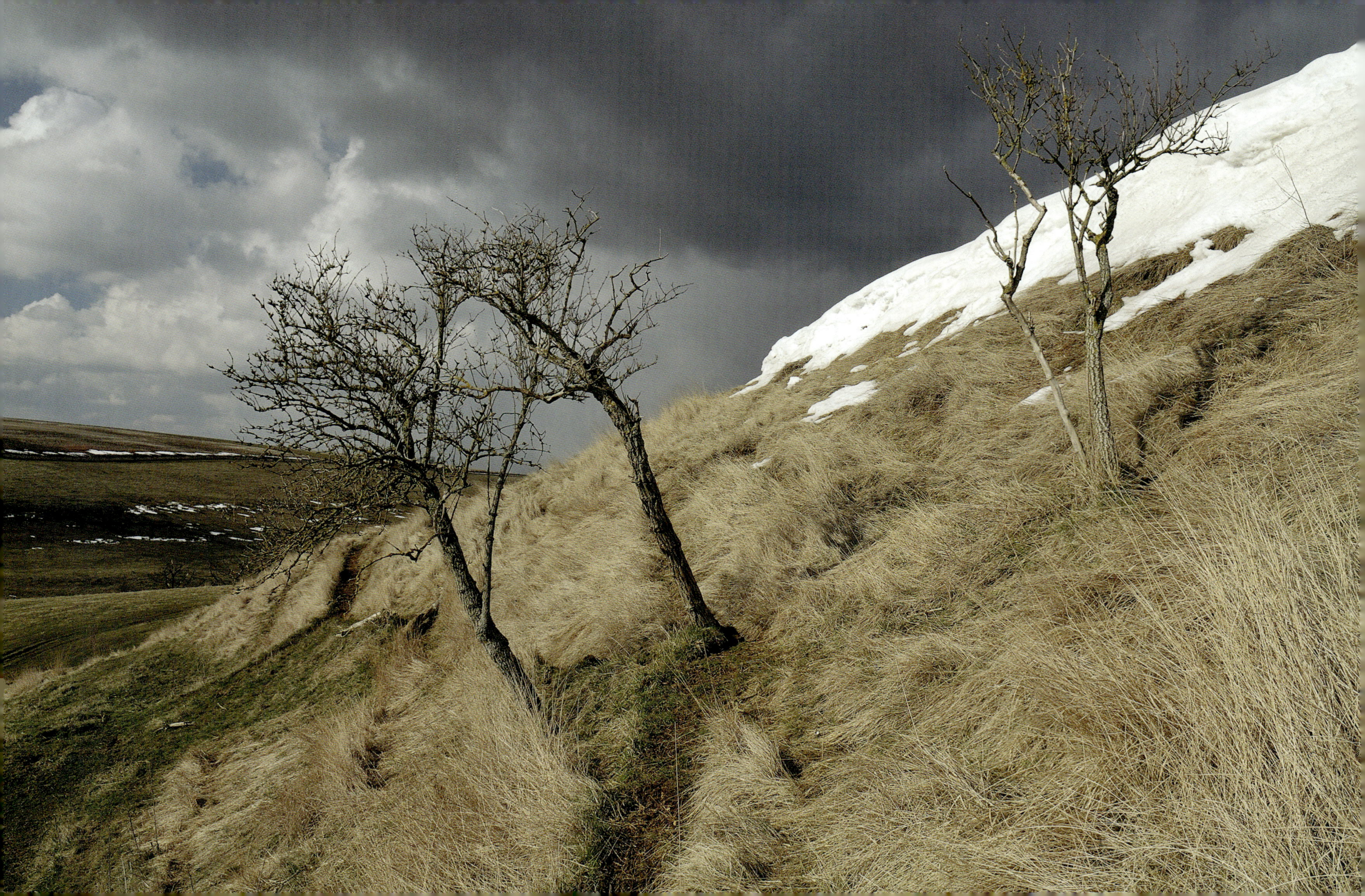

4 : Perceptions

Ah Lincolnshire, all fens, flats and fogs! (George III)

...if the scenery be resolutely level, insisting on the declaration of its flatness in all the detail of it, as in...Lincolnshire...it appears to me like a prison, and I cannot long endure it. (from Mountain Glory, John Ruskin, 1860)

I come from haunt of coot and hern, I make a sudden sally, And sparkle out among the fern, To bicker down a valley (from The Brook, Alfred Lord Tennyson, 1860s)

Opinions about the Lincolnshire landscape are often divided. Shortly after work started on this book the county was voted the third least attractive in Britain in a national poll, rating lower even than some heavily industrialised areas. This caused mild outrage in the local press but it does suggest that Lincolnshire still suffers from an image problem nationally. Even today its countryside is frequently referred to in pejorative terms as flat, dull, bleak or nothing but arable fields, especially when compared to other parts of the country.

Some of this negative imagery is lodged in the national consciousness where it appears to have accumulated historically based on the comments of various writers and even monarchs. On hearing of the Lincolnshire Rising in 1536, Henry VIII famously labelled the county as "one of the most brute and beastly of the whole realm", though it is uncertain whether the insult was topographic as well as social. The exclamation attributed to George III appears almost sympathetic by comparison, but nevertheless reflects an outsider's view of Lincolnshire that is essentially focused on the inner Fens – still only partially drained at the time – and the lurid descriptions of that area by contemporary writers who portrayed it as a dangerous wilderness of malarial swamps and restive natives. Such accounts made little or no reference to the advanced and prosperous

FACING PAGE: **Nettleton Beck, Lincolnshire Wolds**

RIGHT: **dawn over Wingland Marsh, Fens**

agricultural society of the Townlands and Fen edges, which had existed for centuries and produced some of England's finest church architecture. A legacy of oft-repeated prejudices among those with little or no direct experience of Lincolnshire may therefore explain some of the negative perceptions of its landscape today. However, it is not the whole picture, as some visitors and even some residents find little to praise and the Fens in particular can still evoke a response bordering on phobia in some people.

Contrasting with these negative views there are many people who express a deep appreciation and even love for the Lincolnshire landscape. Such sentiments often refer to its unsurpassed sense of space, its subtle beauty and variety and the rich natural and historical legacy that frames and transcends its present use for intensive farming. Lincolnshire's landscape has had few famous advocates through history, though Tennyson's poetry and the paintings of Peter de Wint clearly draw on the area for inspiration.

These differing perceptions of the Lincolnshire landscape are worth exploring further, as they will influence how it is valued and managed into the future in the face of increasing pressure for development and environmental change. The perception of landscape is a complex issue that is influenced by both the inherent qualities of the landscape and the cultural views of the observer. For simplicity, however, this chapter focuses on the twin complaints of flatness and agricultural dominance, which go to the heart of landscape value in Lincolnshire. Overall, the chapter seeks to understand and challenge some of the negative perceptions of Lincolnshire and hopefully increase appreciation of its landscape.

Topographic Notions: Flatness, Intimacy & the Sublime

The flatness of Lincolnshire is part real and part myth. As guidebooks and tourist brochures invariably point out, Lincolnshire is not as flat as its reputation suggests, being crossed by the upland belts of the Jurassic limestone and the Lincolnshire Wolds, both of which rise to around 500 ft (152m) at their highest points. The Wolds, especially, have a hilly landscape that is justly celebrated for its distinctive beauty of contouring. However, care is needed here to avoid an apologism in which the Wolds are presented

LEFT: **Stoke Rochford, Kesteven Uplands**

FACING PAGE: **farmed landscape in summer, Toft-next-Newton**

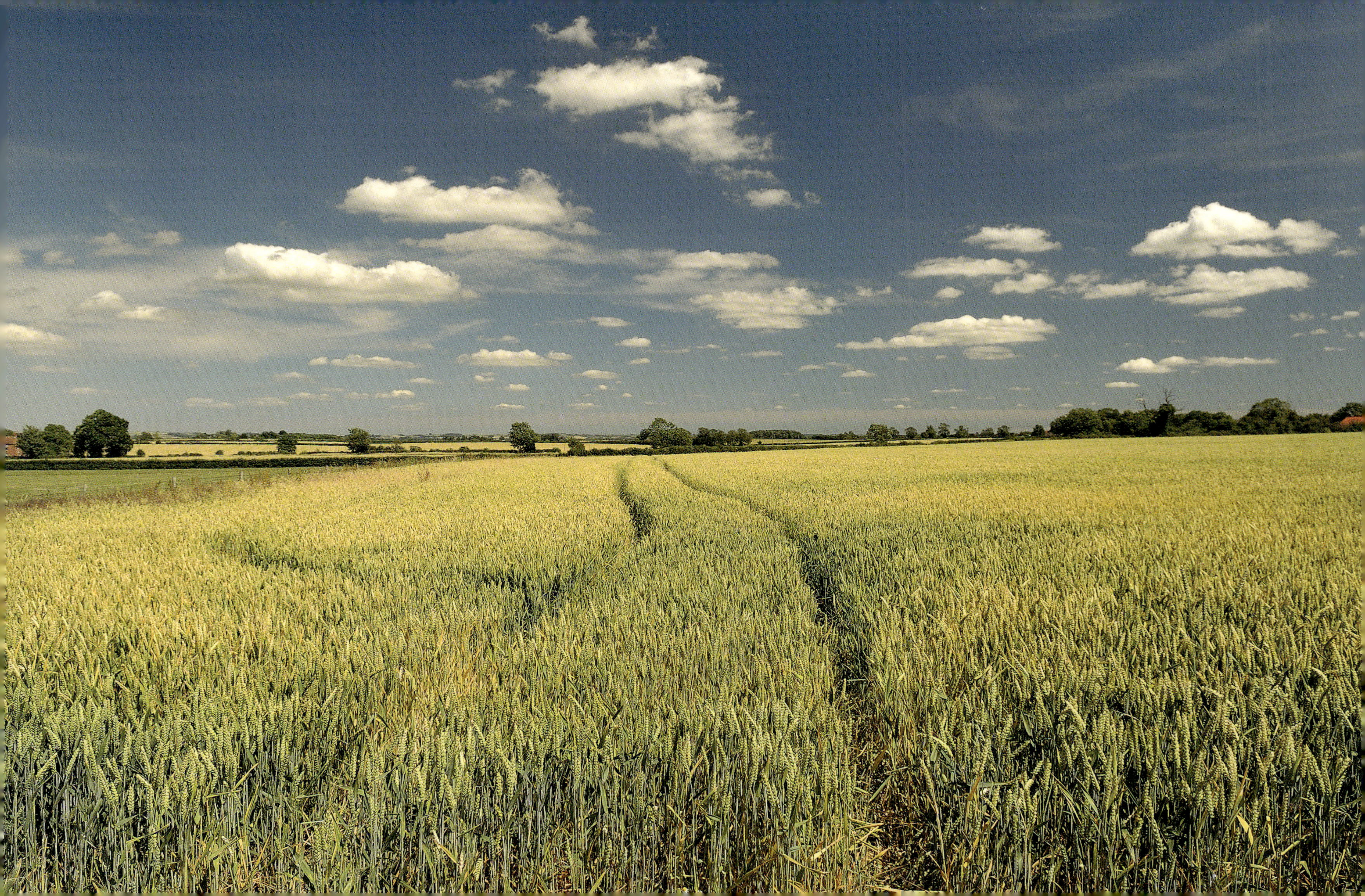

as making amends topographically for the rest of Lincolnshire's countryside, which is thereby dismissed as too flat, uninteresting and inferior. Lincolnshire is not all flat but large tracts of it undeniably are, including all the former wetlands and most of the clay vales. Flatlands are an integral part of Lincolnshire both ecologically and culturally and deserve to be considered and appreciated in their own right. The classic case is the Fens, where the absence of contours frames the whole experience of landscape, allowing vast skies and unbounded horizons that can be exhilarating and at times highly dramatic, especially when thunderstorms cross the open expanses.

The Wolds and Fens represent the polar extremes of relief, but both share a sweeping quality that is arguably the true determinant of Lincolnshire's landscape. Above all, its topography is gradual in nature and only occasionally has rapid contouring or sudden breaks. Even the uplands are characterised more by plateau expanses and smoothly rolling forms than by precipitous slopes and are seldom deeply enclosing. The escarpments of the Lincoln Edge and Wolds are exceptions, but these have the effect of reinforcing the sweep of the landscape by giving elevation and points of focus, while

Beauty in flatness? Flat landscapes in England have generally been accorded a lower value and less official protection than upland areas and hills. By contrast many Lincolnshire residents have long appreciated flatness, with its open skies and sweeps, as a key part of the county's character and appeal.

LEFT: **near Torksey, Vale of Trent**

FACING PAGE: **stormclouds over Asendyke, Fens**

57

The Wolds possess the boldest relief in Lincolnshire. Away from the bounding scarps and main valleys, however, the prevailing character is smoothly undulating and sweeping as in these scenes **near Burwell** (LEFT) and **near Withcall** (BELOW).

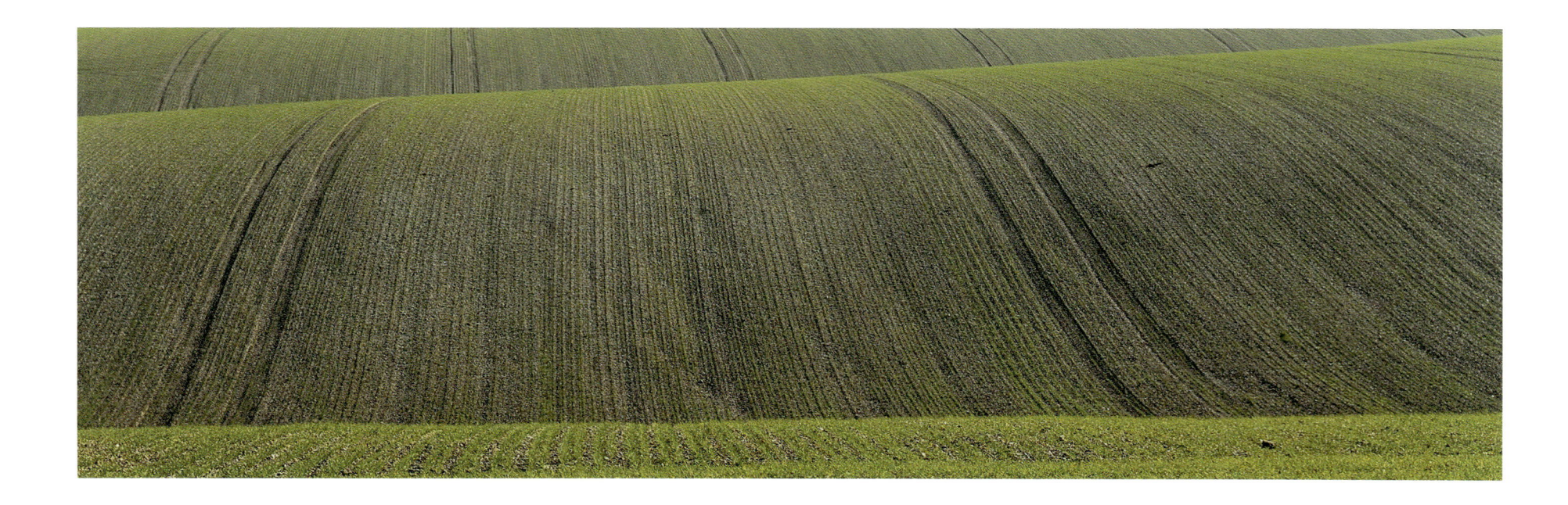

The Lincolnshire countryside is typically open and spacious yet also intimate and even secretive. The latter qualities are found in all of Lincolnshire's landscapes to some extent but are most apparent where there are more hedges or woods.

ABOVE: **old pasture with oaks, Stroxton**

RIGHT: **green lane in the Kesteven Fen edge, Scopwick**

also being dramatised beyond their real height by wide separation and the lack of competing topographic features.

Lincolnshire's expansive quality is amplified by the openness of much of the farmed landscape. Typically, this has large fields and is modestly provided with hedges and woodland that would otherwise restrict views. Field amalgamation and hedgerow removal are partly responsible but not entirely so, as much of the countryside was relatively open even before these changes. Lincolnshire has its more enclosed and wooded areas but the prevailing mood is expansive rather than cosy or bosky. In some ways it is still closer to the vast landscapes of open field agriculture than to the typical, well-hedged English countryside of enclosure. Some people experience this openness as bleakness, especially when it combines with the relative flatness of the landscape. However, such perceptions have evolved through history and, arguably, may reflect an established cultural preference for hillier or more wooded scenery rooted in the Romantic

Lincolnshire Sublime? Lincolnshire has virtually none of the wildly rugged scenery made popular from the late 18th century by Romantic artists and writers such as John Ruskin. The scarp of the Wolds between Tealby and Nettleton is the county's only real attempt at upland grandeur, including the hoary, almost Pennine valley of **Nettleton Beck** (ABOVE). However, Lincolnshire is not without its own drama in the sweeping expanses and immense skies and can be awe-inspiring when the expansive landscape provides the setting for stormclouds, as here in the Wolds at **Wyham Top** (FACING PAGE).

tradition of landscape appreciation. Starting in the late 18th century, this saw landscape beauty primarily in the 'sublime' (awesomely wild) and the picturesque, and largely supplanted preceding notions of attractiveness based on agricultural productiveness. Romantic tastes remain a key arbiter of landscape value today, as seen in landscape designations such as National Parks and Areas of Outstanding Natural Beauty. Simultaneously, the hedged countryside created by enclosure that John Clare railed against in his poetry in the early 19th century has ironically become a familiar and even popular norm that many people now seek to protect from change.

Lincolnshire lacks the wild drama of mountains, crags and gorges popularized by the Romantic movement and instead requires a different landscape aesthetic that celebrates space and light, closer to Turner's art than to Wordsworth or Ruskin. Here, the land is frequently subservient to the sky. Cloudscapes are seen at their fullest and finest and individual landscape components such as trees and buildings become isolated and intensified under the vast heavens. Visually, it often has more in common with the open landscapes of northern France, and occasionally even the American Midwest, than the 'patchwork quilt' ideal of rural England.

Conversely, though, Lincolnshire's openness should not be exaggerated, as there is paradoxically also an intimacy in the landscape, which is far from being a featureless plain or 'prairie'. This human scale is provided by the wealth of natural and historic detailing, including the trees, hedges, lanes and watercourses and the wildlife that these support. Even in the most open parts of the Fens, the reeds, dragonflies and birds of the drainage channels offer an intimate counterpoint to the skyey vastness.

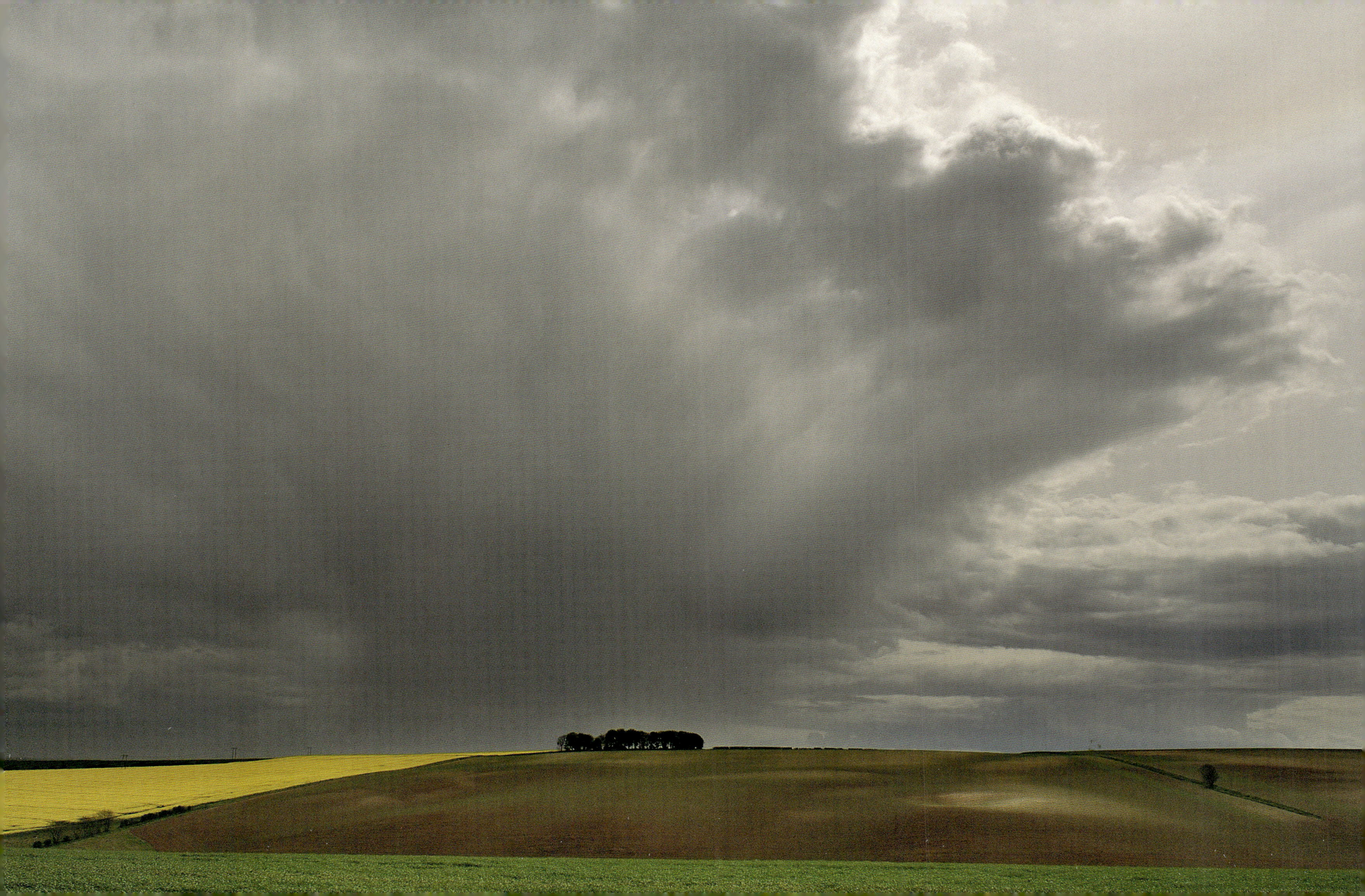

Agriculture & Landscape Beauty

The second frequent complaint against the Lincolnshire landscape is its domination by farming. Lincolnshire has been a leader in agricultural innovation for two centuries and remains so today, presenting a countryside of intensive production rather than quaint rusticity. Additionally, as elsewhere in eastern England, there has been the historic shift since World War II from mixed farming to arable production based on heavy machinery and chemical inputs, with dramatically less land under pasture and meadow. For some, the resulting landscape is an agricultural factory floor in which all natural beauty has been sacrificed to the growing of crops. Again, however, such perceptions warrant further scrutiny.

The ecological losses from agriculture in Lincolnshire have undeniably been massive and lamentable whether or not they were justified historically to feed Britain's growing population. Away from the coastline with its wild dunes, salt marshes and mudflats, there is a scattering of ancient woodlands and a few precious fragments of heathland and bog, but little else has escaped reclamation for farming over the centuries. Today, countryside in Lincolnshire overwhelmingly means farmland and its constituent fields, hedges, trees and wildlife. However, this is far from unique to Lincolnshire and could equally be said of many cherished English landscapes such as the South Downs and Cotswolds and even the dales of the Pennines.

Lincolnshire's particular stigma seems to be the dominance and intensity of arable farming across much of its area and reflects a widespread cultural preference in England for more pastoral or mixed countryside. This may be based on the upland location of most pasture nationally and its greater suitability for ramblers but again points to the aesthetic legacy of the Romantic movement, which tended to admire pastoral scenes as natural, timeless and picturesque. In William Blake's poem *Milton* (1808), for instance, the "Holy Lamb of God" walks anciently on England's mountains and pastures but seemingly avoids the fields of wheat and barley that had been a part of the landscape since the Neolithic period. While images of harvesting and ploughing have held an enduring appeal in English art

LEFT: **pastoral landscape near Kirmond-le-Mire, Wolds**

FACING PAGE: **tulip field, Weston Hills, Fens**

and culture alongside pastoral themes, arable farmland as a whole is still widely seen as artificial, mundane or purely commercial, especially in its modern, highly mechanised form. But are Lincolnshire's arable landscapes necessarily of lesser value and unworthy of aesthetic appreciation?

Crop monocultures over wide areas are certainly monotonous, but a variety of crops is more usual in Lincolnshire, where they give colour and texture to the landscape and form blocks, stripes and lines that emphasise the contours and field patterns. The near mathematical precision of modern cultivation beds and drilling can produce striking visual effects that simultaneously reflect the natural environment (soils, landforms and so on) and contrast with its wildness. There is often a strange beauty in this marriage of nature and geometry. The arable landscape is also highly dynamic; fields change in appearance in response to the seasons, farming practices and economics, and particular scenes differ dramatically from year to year depending on the crops being grown.

Individually, some Lincolnshire crops do have an established visual appeal. Fields of barley have long been admired as a feature of the county and, though the tulip fields around Spalding have all but disappeared in recent decades, daffodils still provide intense colour that attracts visitors to the Fens in spring. Other crops are rarely celebrated in this way – wheat, beans, potatoes, cabbages, turnips, sugar beet, celery and so on – but each makes its own landscape contribution and has its own local history and geography.

Ploughed soils are the other defining element of the arable aesthetic. These reveal beautifully the diversity and colour of the surface geology and often make a strong contribution to landscape character. Lincolnshire's soils range from brown-black fen peat to the arid paleness of the chalk Wolds.

Lincolnshire may lack the wildness of mountain and moorland scenery or the ancient romance of Britain's pastoral uplands, but its predominantly arable surface provides colour, texture and variety to the landscape. Along with Lincolnshire's sweeping topography and vast skies, agriculture helps to define a countryside that is contemporary and often visually striking, but also locally distinctive, varied and rich in natural and cultural heritage. Hopefully, these landscape qualities will become more widely recognised and appreciated in both popular and official opinion as Lincolnshire faces the pressures and challenges outlined in the next chapter. Such recognition is essential if the county's landscape character and diversity are to be properly valued and conserved for future generations.

The Lincolnshire landscape is a far cry from the rugged scenery of Britain's highlands and also lacks the picturesqueness of East Anglia, yet it possesses its own distinctive beauty in the varied and changing interplay between land, sky, wildlife and people.

FACING PAGE, LEFT: **near Stainton-le-Vale, Wolds**

FACING PAGE, RIGHT: **Small-leaved lime, Bardney Limewoods**

ABOVE: **Asgarby and Ewerby spires, Kesteven Fen edge**

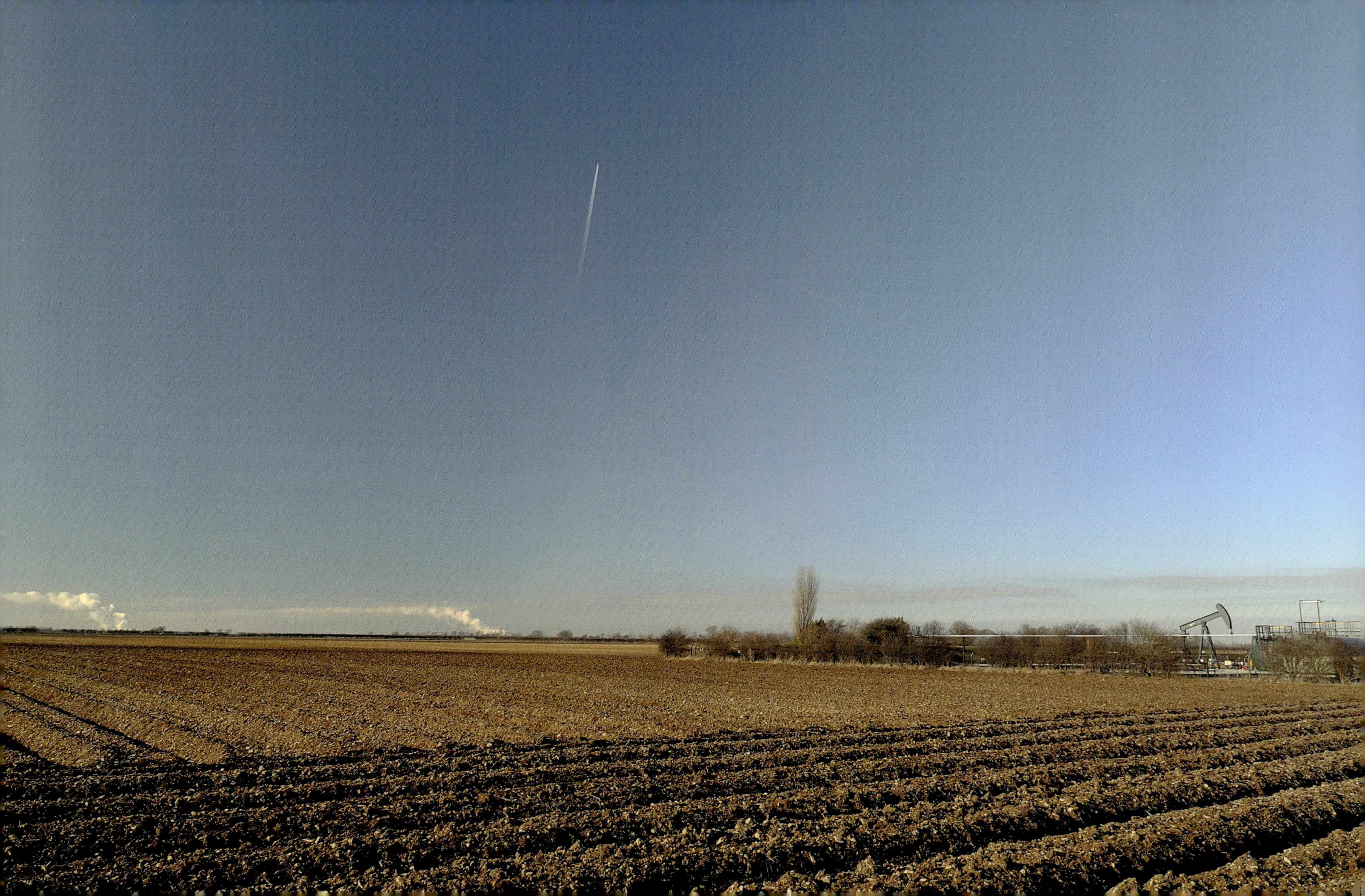

5 : The Future

The landscape of Lincolnshire has changed dramatically throughout history and will undoubtedly continue to evolve in the future. This chapter provides a brief overview of the main factors that are expected to influence its use and appearance over the coming decades. It does not attempt to define a vision for the countryside, but seeks to augment this book as a whole in promoting the conservation of landscape value – ecological, historic and aesthetic – as a key objective for a sustainable future.

Climate Change & Energy

Climate change is already affecting the UK and is predicted to have significant implications for Lincolnshire and its landscape even if international cuts in greenhouse gas emissions can be agreed and delivered to limit global warming. Changing weather patterns, including greater volatility of rainfall and temperature, are already impacting on both agriculture and wildlife and creating new ecologies. The growing and flowering seasons for crops and wild plants are shifting along with the distribution, migration and breeding patterns of birds and other fauna. There are likely to be winners and losers as environmental conditions favour certain species and push out others. Generally, natural ecosystems and growing zones for crops are expected to experience a northward shift as average temperature rises, with Lincolnshire becoming progressively more like present-day southern England and then France. Some scenarios foresee a Mediterranean climate within decades if current trends continue unchecked. However, the added complexities of the North Atlantic Drift

FACING PAGE: **winter morning, Welton Cliff.** Fossil fuels currently play a major role in Lincolnshire's landscape. As well as the oil well on the right of this scene, the plumes of two coal-fired power stations can be seen on the horizon and aircraft contrails overhead. The intensive arable farming typical of the area requires large amounts of fossil energy for farm machinery and artificial fertilisers. It seems unlikely that these energy patterns can be sustained into the future as the UK decarbonises its economy to tackle the threat of global warming.

RIGHT: **sunflower in wildlife strip, Wellingore Heath**

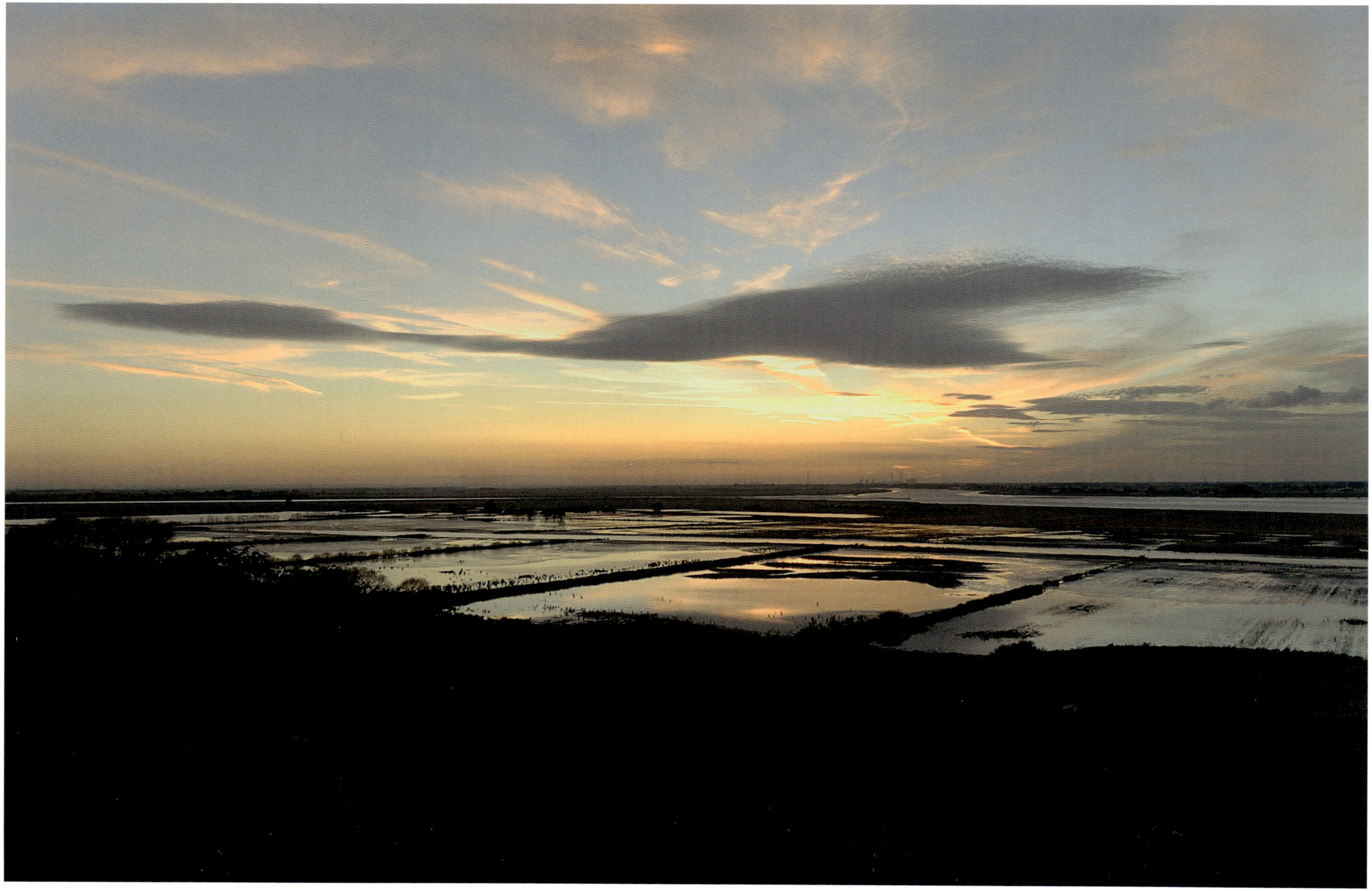

and jet stream and how these respond to polar melting may paradoxically leave Britain with colder winters and/or wetter summers even as the planet warms overall.

Rising sea levels and greater storminess are another aspect of climate change that is predicted to affect Lincolnshire through increased flood risk in coastal areas and river floodplains. Some commentators have suggested that the cost of sea defences and lowland drainage will ultimately become uneconomic and require a managed retreat on a large scale. In one such scenario most of the Fens would return to something like their undrained state in response to a marine advance last seen in pre-Saxon times. Clearly, this would take Lincolnshire into uncharted territory, with massive social

FACING PAGE: **sunset from Trent Cliff near Alkborough.** Managed retreat to allow flooding along major rivers and the coastline is increasingly recognised as the best response to rising sea levels and flood risk, as seen in these fields beside the River Humber at Alkborough Flats. The confluence of the Rivers Trent and Ouse to form the Humber can be seen in the distance.

RIGHT: **ash tree, South Common, Lincoln.** Of all the landscape changes facing Lincolnshire, the expected impact of the Ash dieback fungus (*Chalara fraxinea*) may prove to be one of the most significant in the short to medium term. Ash currently predominates as a hedgerow and woodland tree over large parts of Lincolnshire and is predicted to suffer 60 to 95 per cent losses based on the experience in Denmark and elsewhere in Europe. In the longer term, individual trees with resistance to the fungus may allow the gradual repopulation of ash in the landscape. Climate change and the growth of global trade are thought to be the main factors in the increasing number of tree diseases affecting Britain over the last decade.

and economic consequences, but the geological and archaeological records contain a warning that the relatively fixed coastline of recent centuries has coincided with a period of unusually stable sea levels. Localised managed retreat has already occurred in places on the coast and along rivers as part of strategies to manage flood risk and create wildlife habitats.

Measures to reduce greenhouse gas emissions represent a further driver for landscape change. The need for low carbon energy is likely to translate

ABOVE: **wind farm at Conisholme Fen, Lincolnshire Marsh.** Wind turbines are a source of major controversy and opposition in Lincolnshire as elsewhere in the UK, with public opinion divided on whether they enhance or detract from the character of the landscape.

into more land under biomass and biofuel crops. Wood, straw, osier and Miscanthus are already established as biomass crops and current EU policies on biofuels are boosting oilseed rape as elsewhere in Britain.

Wind energy is controversial but ultimately seems likely to increase as carbon cuts become more pressing. Lincolnshire has ten commercial onshore wind farms operating at the time of writing, all located in the Fens, Marsh and the Scunthorpe area, where they have a significant though fairly localised visual impact. However, the openness of Lincolnshire's countryside arguably makes it more sensitive to wind development, presenting a major challenge for the planning system in balancing aesthetic concerns with the need for Lincolnshire to play its part in delivering a low carbon future.

Commercial solar generation has grown rapidly in Lincolnshire in recent years and several large schemes are already operating. Solar farms offer a

TOP RIGHT: **oilseed rape near Thoresway, Wolds.** The brilliant yellow bloom of this crop caused much opposition in the UK in the 1980s when it was criticized for being alien and damaging to the traditional landscape. Today it has become widely accepted by the public and is now popular with many for its vibrant colour in spring. However, there are new concerns that it is becoming overdominant in some areas and that its use for biofuel is removing land from food production and driving the loss of traditional pasture. Rapeseed has an established history in Lincolnshire as 'coleseed', having been introduced into the Fens from the Netherlands in the 17th century.

RIGHT: **Miscanthus or 'elephant grass' near Cold Hanworth.** The growing of crops for biofuel and biomass is already altering Lincolnshire's landscape. Other novel energy and food crops are likely to appear in Lincolnshire as climate change progresses.

'low rise' alternative to wind farms that is suited to Lincolnshire's sunny climate, though loss of land for crops and biomass, as well as landscape impacts, are potential issues if major expansion occurs. Smaller-scale renewable generation by local communities and individuals is another strand of the low carbon approach, with wind, solar and biomass each offering opportunities for decentralised energy.

Despite global warming, the UK Government appears likely to pursue the increased domestic production of onshore oil and gas, including the exploitation of shale gas by hydraulic fracturing ('fracking'). Oil extraction has occurred in Lincolnshire since the 1940s in the Gainsborough and Welton areas, with limited visual impact. However, Lincolnshire has large estimated reserves of oil and shale gas that are facing growing pressure for extraction, with potentially significant impacts for landscapes and communities. Key concerns include traffic during construction and drilling, damage to aquifers and water pollution, as well as visual intrusion.

Farming Futures

Lincolnshire's agricultural future may be framed by climate change but also faces other challenges and choices. Alternative visions exist that range from a widespread move to organic farming and more localised food production through to high-tech farming based on GM crops and further intensification. Simultaneously, measures to reverse declines in biodiversity will require successful integration with farming regimes. Lincolnshire is likely to be at the forefront of these debates, as seen in the recent proposal for a 'superdairy' at Nocton. Along with carbon reduction targets, the future availability of oil may ultimately determine whether farming can continue on its current high energy path or is effectively forced into alternative approaches analogous to Cuba's green response to the US-led oil embargo. The conservation of landscape and its natural and cultural value should, however, remain a central aim whatever system of farming is pursued.

LEFT: **solar photovoltaic array, North Rauceby**

FACING PAGE: **wildflower strip on farmland near Skillington.** Major progress has been made since the 1980s in integrating farming and wildlife in Lincolnshire including planting of hedgerows and woodland and the introduction of wildlife and game strips along field margins to provide food and shelter. Hopefully, the forthcoming reform of EU agricultural policies will allow such ecological approaches to be consolidated and extended to benefit wildlife and the public.

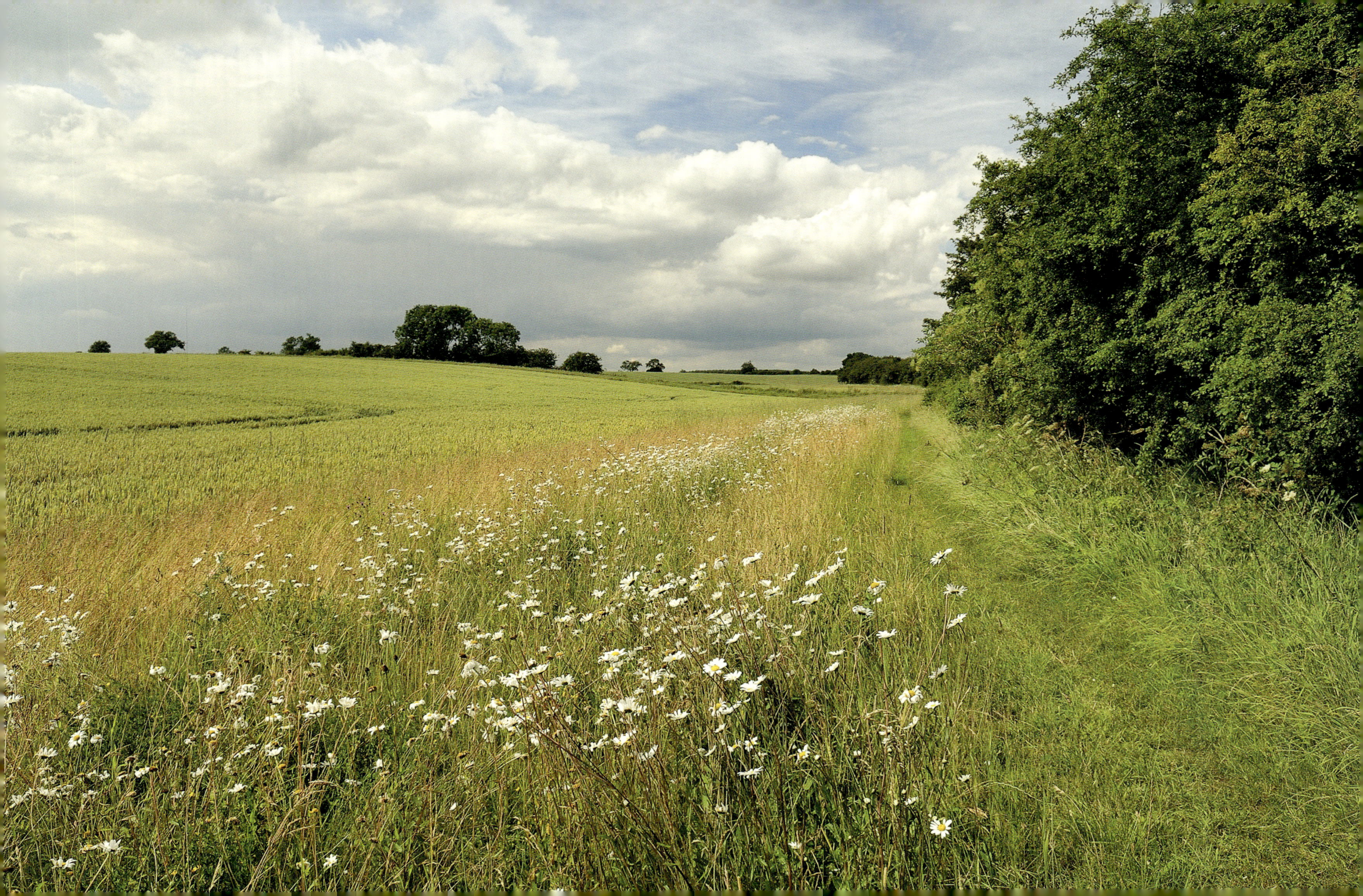

Population & Development

Despite perceptions of peripherality, Lincolnshire has experienced rapid population growth from in-migration in recent decades, leading to increased pressure for new housing and employment as well as additional infrastructure including new roads. Many rural settlements have seen significant expansion and traffic levels have increased due to commuting and leisure trips. Population growth is predicted to continue as people are attracted to Lincolnshire by its relatively low housing costs and rural environment. Again, the planning system has a key role in managing these growth pressures to meet people's economic and social needs while conserving the character and quality of Lincolnshire's environment. The overall level of new development and how well it is designed and integrated with the landscape will be key considerations to ensure that environmental quality is not sacrificed in the pursuit of growth.

Diversification of the local economy is another key objective of plans for Lincolnshire's future, with the rural economy identified as an important growth sector. There are clear opportunities to link this to Lincolnshire's established role in food production, with an emphasis on high quality local produce that supports landscape conservation objectives.

Tourism & Leisure

Lincolnshire is attracting more visitors than ever before, with the countryside becoming increasingly popular as a destination alongside the established coastal resorts. The county's location and relatively subdued

ABOVE: **new rural housing near Lincoln.** Architectural quality is partly a matter of taste, but sustainable development needs to be sympathetic to its landscape setting as well as meeting high standards of environmental performance. Despite a growing awareness of design in recent years, some new housing developments in Lincolnshire still seem poorly related to local landscape character, indicating that a more robust approach is needed in the design and planning process.

Growth and infrastructure – how much, where and what? The Lincoln area exemplifies the difficult balance between development and environmental quality as manifested in the landscape. Growth plans for the city aim to boost homes and jobs in accessible locations but will inevitably encroach into the surrounding countryside. Bypass proposals east and south of Lincoln have attracted relatively little opposition by national standards but involve signficant impacts on valued landscapes. The proposed Southern Bypass would cut through open countryside for several miles near the city, including the important scenic and recreational area of the **Lincoln Edge** (FACING PAGE).

75

landscape make it unlikely to experience visitor pressure comparable to popular sites in, say, the Peak District. However, increasing tourism and countryside recreation are impacting on Lincolnshire's countryside, with more holiday accommodation and pressure for new attractions and public access. Public footpaths in Lincolnshire are generally rather sparse and disjointed, reflecting the historical legacy of enclosure. Open access land is also rare due to intensive agriculture. Agreements with landowners for permissive footpaths have, however, expanded rapidly in recent years and it is hoped that this trend will continue to extend public access in future.

Landscape Protection

Statutory protection for landscapes comes from a range of sources, including international conventions and EU directives (e.g. Ramsar sites); various national and local designations for areas and sites based on their value for wildlife, heritage and landscape beauty or amenity; and more general planning policies controlling the location and design of development. The latter have historically restricted building in areas defined as 'open countryside', though the new national planning policy framework issued in 2012 may have shifted the balance in favour of development.

Protecting officially designated areas and sites remains crucial for landscape conservation, but has been criticised in recent years for focusing attention and resources too much on 'special' features at the expense of the character and quality of the wider landscape. Landscape characterisation has started to address this concern and now seeks a proactive and partnership-based approach to maintain and enhance the character of all landscapes. In nature conservation too the focus is broadening from individual nature reserves to landscape-scale conservation and ecological networks. It is hoped that these new approaches will be successfully integrated with the planning sytem and other aspects of land management to help conserve more of Lincolnshire's landscape and its ecological and historic value.

Overall, it is difficult to predict the combined outcome of these factors on the Lincolnshire landscape and how it will appear and function in the future. With sympathetic planning and management, however, it should retain its diverse character and appeal for residents and visitors through the 21st century and beyond while reflecting a sustainable approach to development and change within Lincolnshire as well as globally.

FACING PAGE: **Willow Tree Fen, Deeping St.Nicholas.** This newly established nature reserve lies within one of Lincolnshire's Living Landscape areas which promote a landscape-scale approach to wildlife and landscape conservation. Here, arable farmland between the River Glen and the Counter Drain has been re-wetted and is being managed to recreate habitat for fenland plants and fauna. The site links via the River Glen to Lincolnshire Wildlife Trust's established nature reserves nearby at Baston Fen and Pinchbeck Fen, thereby providing a larger and more ecologically viable area for wildlife. Along with the South Lincolnshire Fenlands, the Trust has identified several other Living Landscape project areas including the Lincolnshire Limestone, Lincolnshire Limewoods and Lincolnshire Wolds. The initiative seeks to protect landscape features of historic and cultural significance alongside ecology.

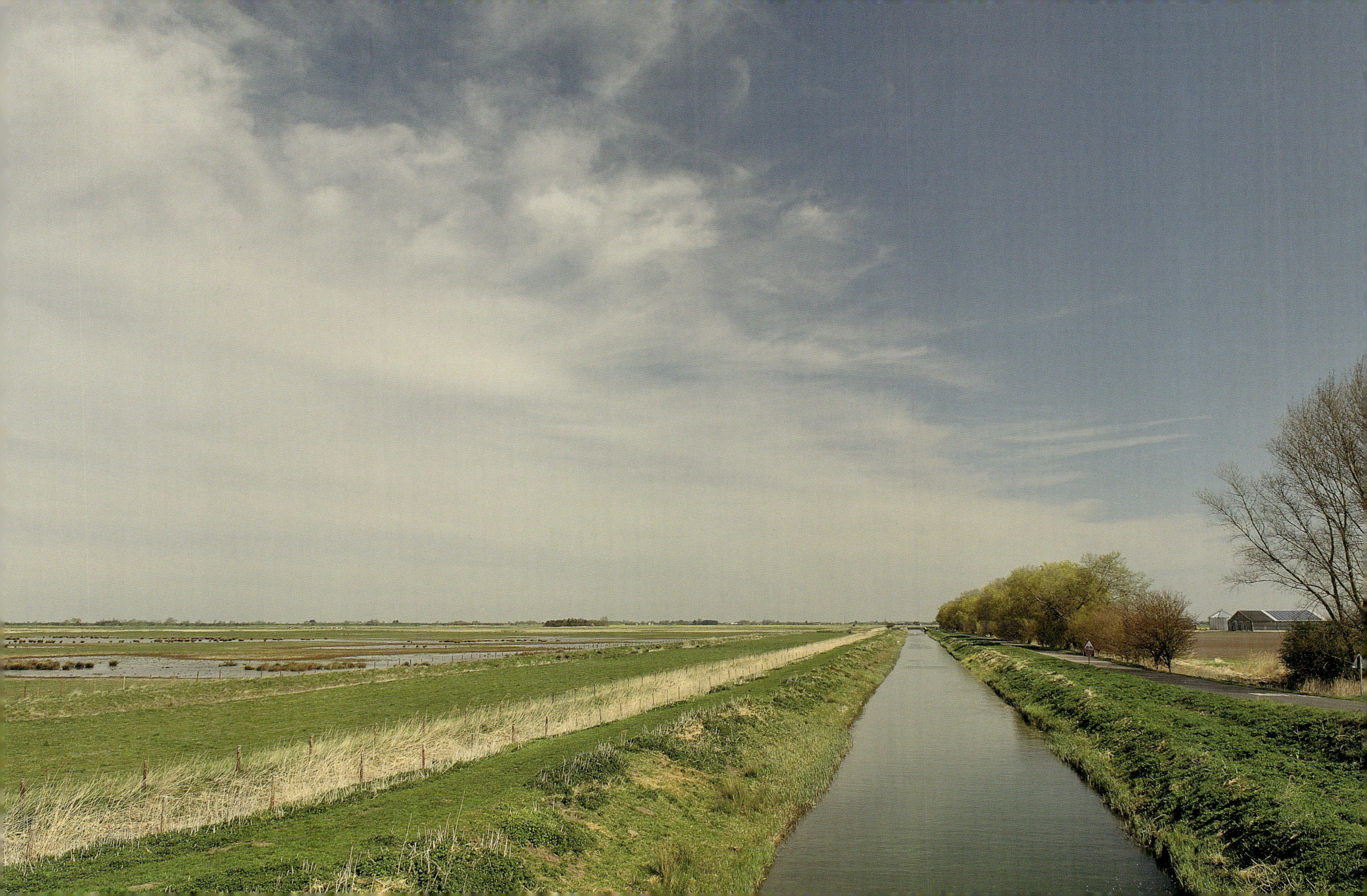

THE LANDSCAPE CHARACTER AREAS

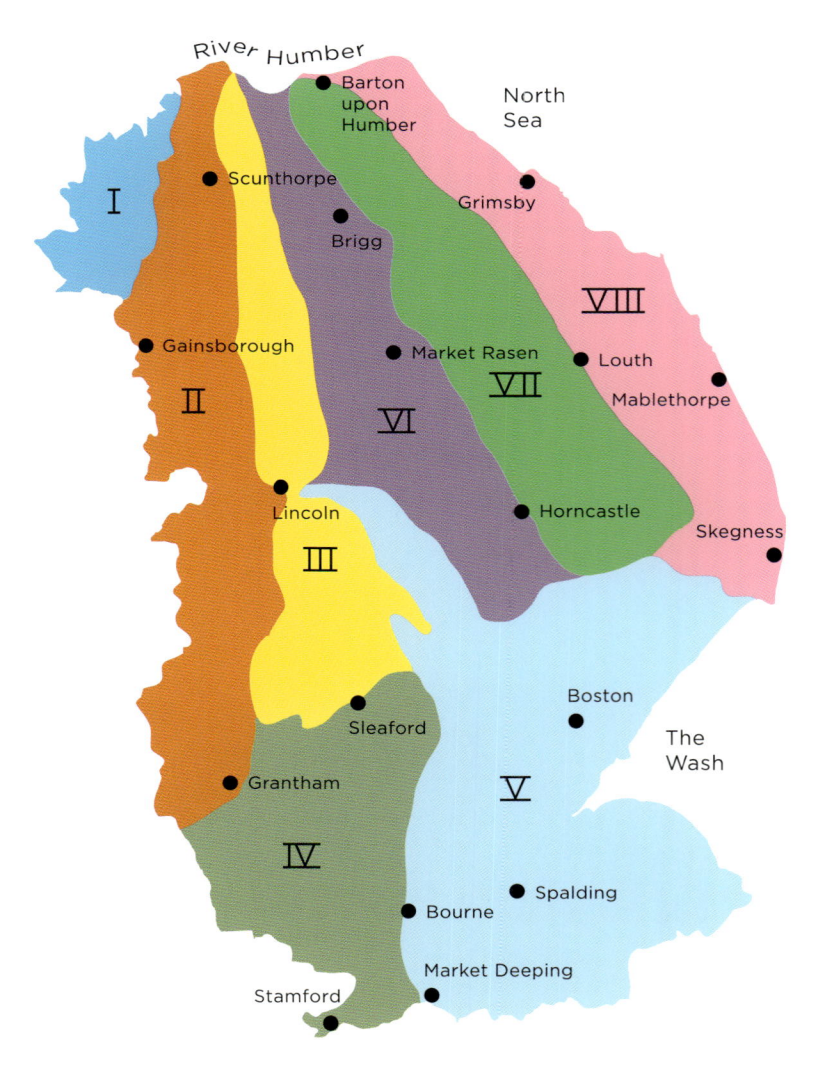

I – Isle of Axholme

The far north-west of Lincolnshire lying west of the River Trent. It forms part of the wider Humberhead Levels which are shared with Yorkshire and Nottinghamshire. It is a historically distinct area based on an island-like ridge of low Triassic hills surrounded by largely reclaimed wetlands of silt and peat. Undrained lowland peat bog survives in places.

II – Vale of Trent

The low-lying clay vale along the western margin of Lincolnshire between the River Trent and the Jurassic limestone ridge to the east. It is shared with Nottinghamshire and has a generally flat relief though with some gentle hills and scarp features provided by harder rocks including Liassic limestones and ironstones. The Trent Valley refers to the river's flood plain and bluffs, which form a distinct corridor landscape within the Vale.

III – Heath & Cliff

The portion of Lincolnshire's Jurassic limestone belt between the Ancaster Gap and the River Humber, characterised by a steep western scarp (the Lincoln Edge) and an open limestone plateau declining slowly eastwards. The name Lincoln Heath refers strictly to the plateau south of Lincoln, though limestone 'heath' also occurred north of Lincoln before the area was fully reclaimed. The whole ridge between Lincoln and the Humber is known locally as the Lincoln Cliff, though confusingly this name is sometimes also applied to the escarpment south of Lincoln.

IV – Kesteven Uplands

The southern portion of Lincolnshire's Jurassic limestone belt. It is a gentle limestone upland dissected by the valleys of the upper Witham and Glen rivers and has more glacial deposits, woodland and pasture than the Heath or Cliff. The upland merges with the limestone plateau of Leicestershire and Rutland on the south-west and subsides gradually to the Welland valley and Stamford in the far south.

V – Fens & The Wash

The Fens are the flat, low-lying area of former wetland around the Wash, extending inland to the Jurassic uplands on the west and the Lincolnshire Wolds on the north. The modern landscape is almost entirely agricultural, based on the historical drainage and reclamation of freshwater fen and coastal marshland. Lincolnshire shares the Fens with the adjoining parts of Peterborough, Cambridgeshire and Norfolk. The Wash is a large coastal embayment with tidal mudflats, sandbanks and deeper channels.

VI – Mid Lindsey Vale

The area of lowland between the Lincoln Cliff and the Lincolnshire Wolds. It is mostly a gently undulating vale based on glacial clay and other deposits, with a flatter area of drained wetlands called 'carrs' along the lower Ancholme valley. The Vale adjoins the Fens on the south, where there is a concentration of ancient limewoods.

RIGHT: **chalk landscape near Thoresway, Wolds**

VII – Lincolnshire Wolds

The upland of Cretaceous rocks that runs across eastern Lincolnshire between the Humber and the Fens. Most of the Wolds are based on chalk, though sandstones and clays form the southern portion between Horncastle and Spilsby. The Wolds are heavily dissected by small streams, creating a succession of valleys, most of which flow eastwards. The upland has a steep western scarp for much of its length and also a steep eastern edge overlooking the Lincolnshire Marsh that marks a former coastal cliff.

VIII – Lincolnshire Marsh & Coast

The lowland coastal plain adjoining the North Sea and Humber estuary. The area is divided between the inland Middle Marsh based on a gently undulating plateau of glacial clay and the coastal Outmarsh of tidal silts. The coastline is mostly sandy with beaches and dune systems, though areas of salt marsh and mudflats occur towards the Humber and the Wash.

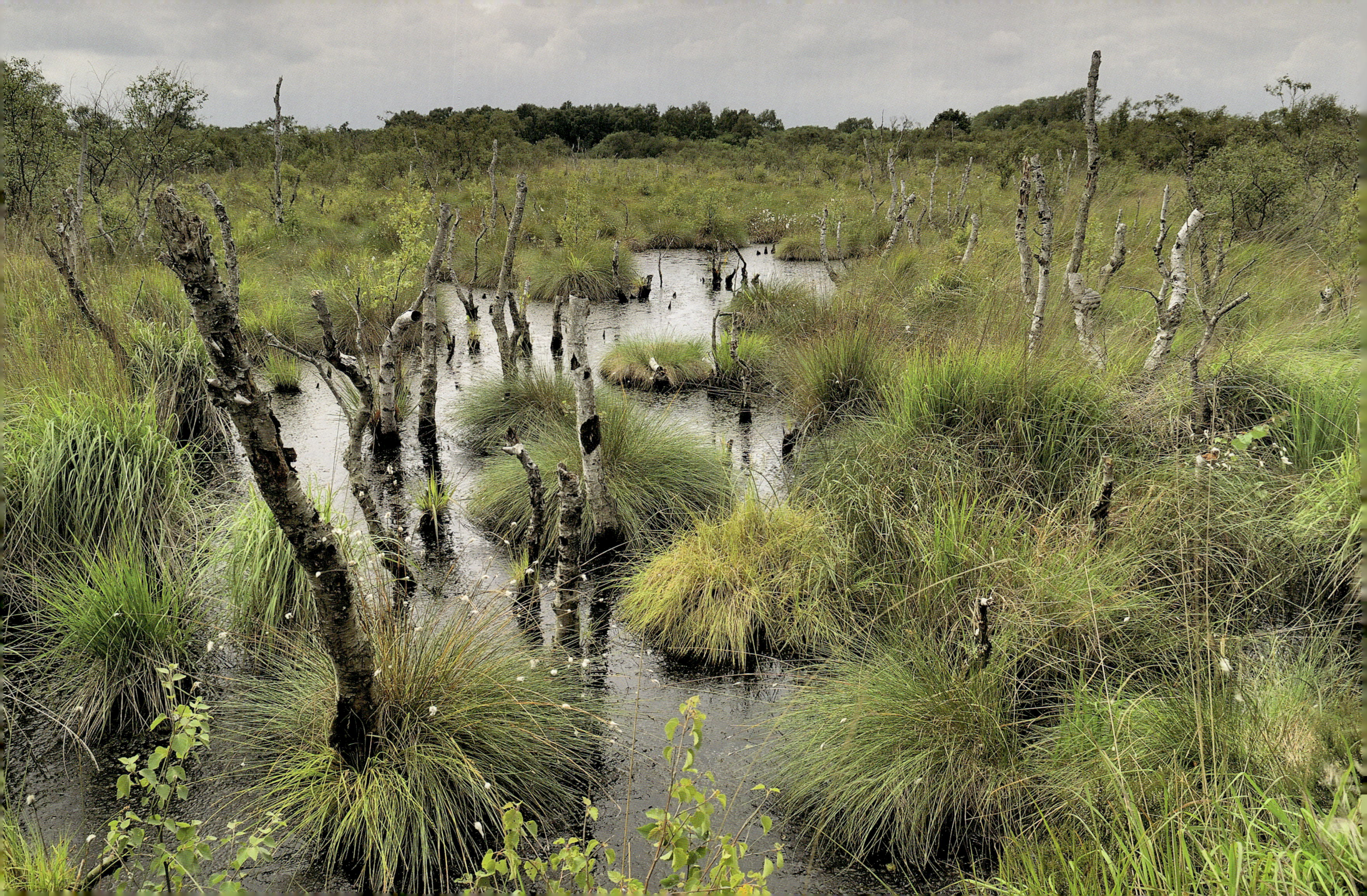

I - ISLE OF AXHOLME

The Isle of Axholme occupies the far north-west of Lincolnshire and is the only part of the historic county lying west of the River Trent. Rather like the better-known Isle of Ely in Cambridgeshire, the 'isle' refers to a physical feature – literally an island of higher ground surrounded by wetlands – but was also a wider territory of Anglo-Saxon or earlier origin defined on all sides by rivers. The name Axholme probably derives from the addition of the Old Norse word 'holm' (island) to Haxey, which is an earlier, Anglo-Saxon name already denoting an island by its 'ey' ending.

The Isle of Axholme is geographically distinct from the rest of Lincolnshire and still retains aspects of its unique history in the landscape and local customs. As explained later, the Isle developed primarily as a landscape of numerous smallholders who were able to defend their interests over larger landowners to an unusual degree. A spirit of robust independence is still reflected in the famous Haxey Hood event which has been held annually between the villages of Haxey and Westwoodside since the 14th century.

Axholme is also unique within Lincolnshire in its proximity to Yorkshire, which adjoins the area on the west. In clear conditions the Pennine hills appear surprisingly close on the western horizon, adding a hint of highland drama that is not found elsewhere in Lincolnshire. The Isle is also said to have historic and cultural ties with Yorkshire, including elements of the local accent, and this has continued in recent decades as Axholme has become a popular commuter and retirement area for south Yorkshire.

The 'island' at the centre of Axholme is composed of Triassic Mercia Mudstone and forms a low, elongated hill with spurs rising from the surrounding flatlands. This provided dry land for settlement and farming to develop while also giving access to the adjoining wetland resources including fish, wildfowl, peat, reeds and grazing. The main villages on the island are Epworth, Haxey and Belton plus their satellites. Two much

FACING PAGE: **Crowle Moor**

RIGHT: **landscape near Epworth**

smaller and lower islands provide the isolated setting for the villages of Crowle and Wroot to the north and west of the main island respectively. The Isle's other villages are situated mainly on the levees of rivers, including the Trent and the old River Don.

Geologically, Axholme's islands are the northern extension of a ridge of Mercia Mudstone that runs from Nottingham to Gringley-on-the-Hill and consequently share the same distinctive pink-red soil colour with Nottinghamshire where ploughed. The flatlands surrounding the islands also have a bedrock of Mercia Mudstone but this has been eroded down, probably by glacial action, and covered by later silts and peat deposits as wetlands developed following the last Ice Age. Coversands were also deposited extensively across the area and remain today on the western flanks of the islands, where they add variety to the landscape and ecology.

The main island of Axholme presents a pleasantly rolling countryside with long views over the flatlands and beyond on all sides. While the red soils are reminiscent of Nottinghamshire, there is an open sparseness in the landscape that suggests Lincolnshire but is also unique to the Isle. Unenclosed open fields and strip-based farming have survived here to a greater extent than anywhere else in England and give the area a highly distinctive character. This is not strictly an untouched fragment of Medieval England, but is nevertheless a remarkable, even alien, landscape today, reflecting the collective ability of Axholme's smallholders to limit outside control of their land and common rights during the enclosure process. Sadly, recent decades have seen the amalgamation of many strips into larger units, leading to gradual erosion of the Isle's identity.

Farming in strips has continued to the present day in several Axholme parishes which retained their Medieval open fields, albeit with major changes in patterns of tenure and farming methods. For example, modern ploughing has removed the characteristic ridging seen elsewhere where open field strips have been 'fossilised' in pasture as ridge and furrow. The landscape of the open fields is increasingly recognised as a unique and valuable part of the Isle's living heritage but faces economic and other pressures for change.

FACING PAGE: **strips near Haxey** (TOP) **and Low Burnham** (BOTTOM)

ABOVE: **an entire landscape of strips from High Burnham towards Haxey**

84

Wetlands and water once surrounded Axholme on all sides and still do on the western boundary with Yorkshire. Here, the lowland peat bogs of Hatfield Moors and Thorne Moors form great expanses of uninhabited land that have been heavily extracted until recently by commercial peat companies but never fully reclaimed. Lincolnshire has its share of this wild wetland area in Crowle Moor, which is managed as a nature reserve and now forms part of the wider Humberhead Peatlands National Nature Reserve with the adjoining Yorkshire peatlands. The area is important for its diversity of species including rare insects and flora and is also home to a breeding population of nightjars. Smaller areas of unreclaimed peatland also survive in the turbaries of Haxey and Epworth which were retained as village commons when the Isle's wetlands were drained and enclosed.

The history of drainage of the Axholme wetlands is complex and closely linked to that of Hatfield Chase in Yorkshire. Some drainage improvements and new canals were completed in the Roman and Medieval periods, but the famous Dutch engineer Cornelius Vermuyden's scheme of the 1620s marked the start of the area's transformation by large-scale drainage, as well as decades of bitter conflict between drainage interests and Axholme's commoners. Reclamation work in Axholme was initially undertaken mainly by foreign settlers, including Walloon and French

FACING PAGE: **evening at Crowle Moor**

TOP RIGHT: **Epworth Turbary**

BOTTOM RIGHT: **winter dawn, Crowle Common**

Huguenot refugees, who had experience of drainage in the Netherlands and established a colony at Sandtoft with Vermuyden. This heightened the clash between the established use of the wetlands as a communal resource and the new capitalist agriculture promoted by the Crown. Alongside protracted lawsuits, the commoners wrecked dykes, sluices, buildings and crops. Rioting, violence and even deaths occurred in battles with the authorities that continued sporadically into the 1700s even after most of the original settlers had departed to work on Vermuyden's drainage schemes elsewhere. Nevertheless, the Axholme commoners ultimately had to accept drainage while receiving a share of drained land as compensation.

As in the Fens, further drainage improvements followed Vermuyden's work to address problems of flooding and peat shrinkage. Steam pumping in the 19th century finally allowed reliable arable farming and Axholme became one of the most productive areas in England, with a high reputation for potatoes and horticultural crops like celery. In places the fertility of the soil was further improved between the 18th and 20th centuries by the deliberate flooding of fields with silty water from the tidal rivers – a process known as 'warping'. This also had the benefit of raising the land surface to reduce the risk of unplanned floods and was sometimes used to reclaim wetland areas.

Vermuyden's drainage scheme involved re-routing all of the area's main rivers except the Trent. The Don was diverted north to the Aire and later

LEFT: **Epworth**

FACING PAGE: **reclaimed peatland, Idle Bank**

87

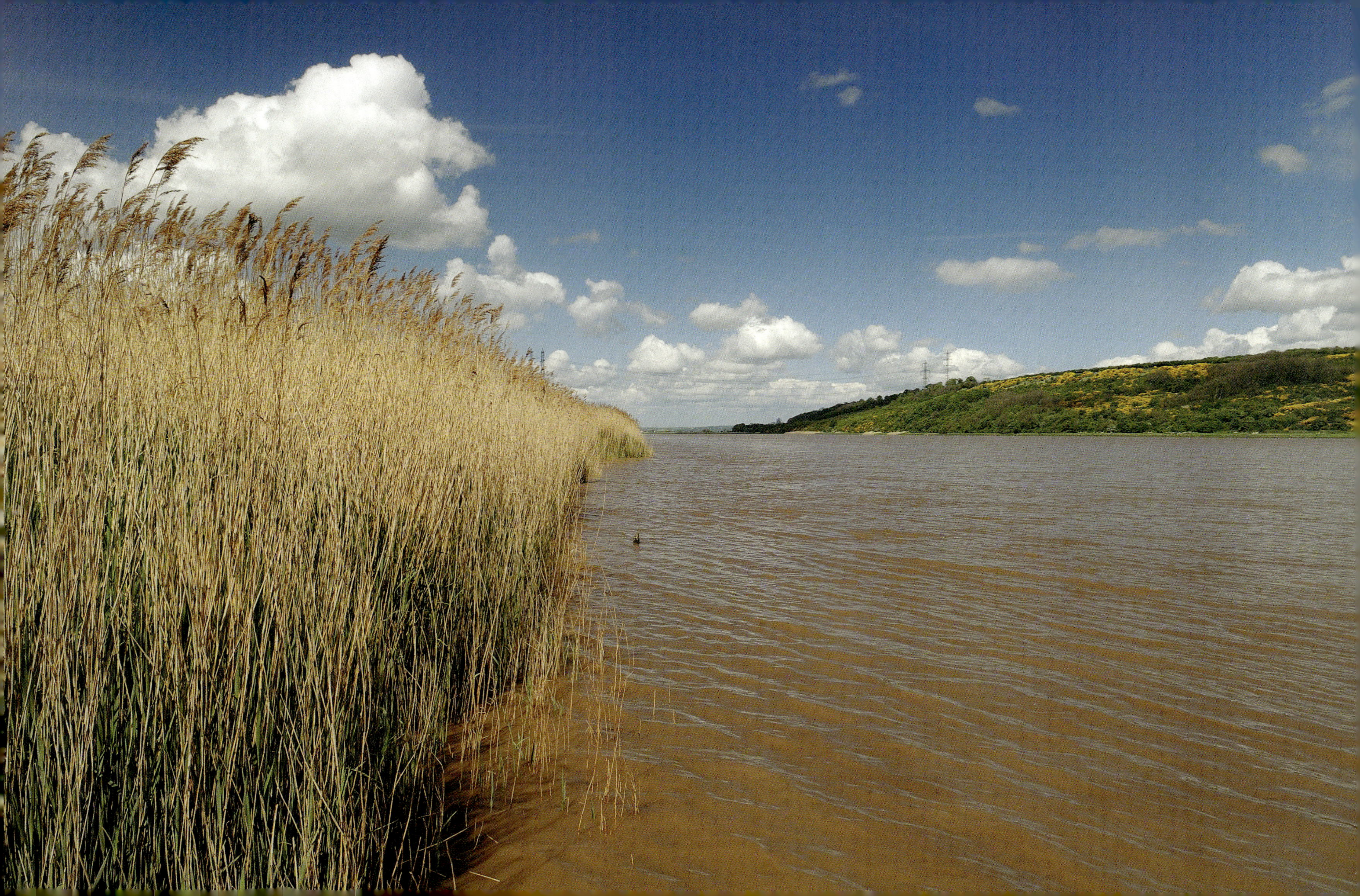

connected directly to the Ouse, and its tributaries the Torne and Idle were rechannelled to the Trent. The former courses of these rivers can still be traced across the landscape in places as field boundaries, ditches and roads. The apparently twinned villages of Garthorpe and Fockerby in the north of Axholme were formerly divided by the River Don which here marked the Medieval boundary with Yorkshire.

Archaeological finds of flint and stone tools indicate that the islands of Axholme were the focus of early human activity and settlement from at least Mesolithic times and almost certainly facilitated exploitation of the surrounding wetlands even as agriculture supplanted hunter-gathering lifestyles. Remains from every period have been found from the Neolithic to the Roman, suggesting continuity of human presence. However, it is unclear whether occupation continued after the Romans departed and the progress of Anglo-Saxon and Danish settlement on Axholme prior to the Domesday Survey is also relatively little understood.

As suggested above, Axholme is of exceptional interest for its history of settlement and enclosure from the Medieval and post-Medieval periods. The unusual, 'polyfocal' pattern seen in the island villages of Belton, Epworth and Haxey originated in the Medieval period and is thought to result from the relatively low level of manorial control, which allowed communities to plan their own environments including the laying out of field systems. The unenclosed open fields of these three parishes represent by far the largest such survival in England, forming a continuous tract along the ridge of the island. The surviving network of paths linking the villages and fields also illustrates the communal nature of traditional farming in this area. Further examples of strip farming are preserved in Axholme's Trentside villages, especially at West Butterwick.

The landscape of Axholme is not untouched by enclosure, however. The Parliamentary enclosure award for the island parishes, while retaining the open fields, enclosed almost all of the remaining commons, leaving only small areas of turbary as compensation for the loss of commoners'

FACING PAGE: **River Trent near Garthorpe**

TOP RIGHT: **trees in open field landscape, High Burnham**

rights. Even before this, most of the former wetlands had been enclosed pursuant to Vermuyden's drainage scheme, and piecemeal enclosure from Medieval times onwards had created a belt of small, private fields and closes on the lower slopes of the main island. Nevertheless, despite the trauma of wetland drainage in the 17th century and subsequent pressures, Axholme's smallholder economy proved resilient and adaptable to change and attracted considerable numbers of economic refugees from surrounding areas impacted by enclosure and rural unemployment. The local hemp and flax industries provided a further draw alongside the availability of land.

Some of the common turbaries subsequently became settlements as smallholdings were let to the poor of the Isle parishes in the 19th century. Settlers typically self-built their cottage dwellings and utilised the land to support themselves with crops and livestock, along with market gardening and digging of sand and peat. Today, a few of these cottages remain in more or less original form as examples of a lowly vernacular architecture that has virtually disappeared elsewhere in Lincolnshire.

Apart from isolated survivals of mud and stud cottage construction, traditional domestic and farm buildings in Axholme are almost all of brick and pantile. Dutch influence can be seen in older brickwork as in other parts of Lincolnshire, though only one or two examples of Dutch gables have survived, such as Epworth post office. Much more common here is the use of stone gable copings and 'kneelers', an architectural feature which the Isle of Axholme shares with parts of Yorkshire.

ABOVE: **Primitive Methodist Chapel, Beltoft.** The Isle of Axholme has an important Methodist heritage as the home of the movement's founders. Both Charles and John Wesley were born in the Isle and grew up in the Old Rectory at Epworth which is now a museum for the Wesleys and Methodism.

FACING PAGE: **Autumn evening near Haxey**

91

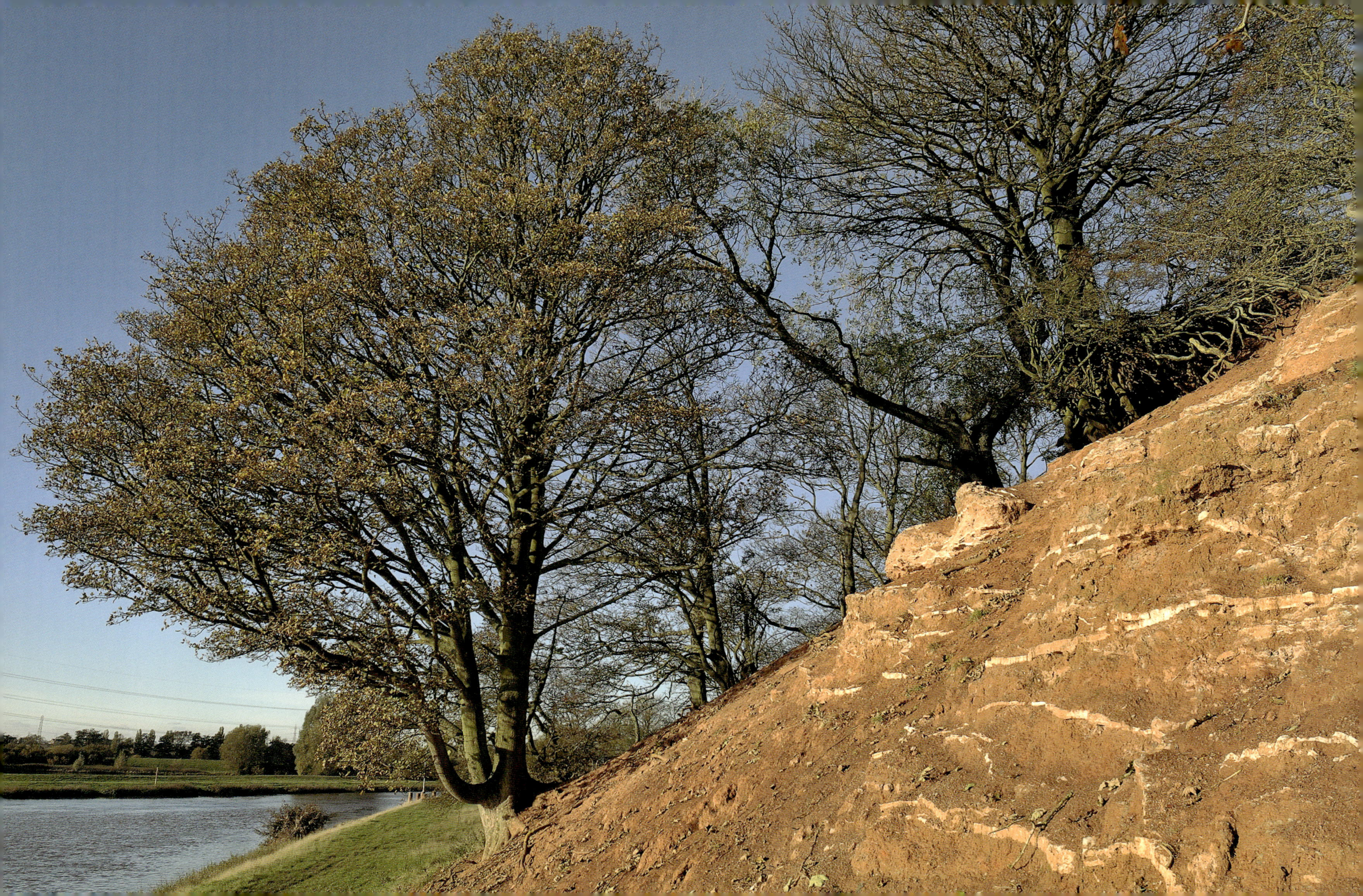

II - VALE OF TRENT

Except in the far north-west corner of Lincolnshire where it crosses the River Trent to encompass the Isle of Axholme, the county's western fringes occupy a broad lowland vale which is shared with Nottinghamshire and known loosely as the Vale of Trent. Much of the Vale actually drains into the River Witham and its tributaries rather than the Trent but there is some justification for the name as explained later. Lengthwise the Vale stretches some 60 miles (97 km) from the neighbouring Vale of Belvoir in the south to the Humber in the north where it merges with the Humberhead Levels.

A good overview of the Vale is available, literally, from the scarp of the Lincoln Edge, which forms a remarkable natural bulwark defining the Vale's eastern limit for most of its length. On a clear day the Vale is seen as a flattish sweep of farmed countryside and woods extending to the shallow Trent Valley, where the cooling towers of coal-fired power stations rise prominently from the far bank of the river. Beyond are gentle, farmed hills which bound the Vale on the west in Nottinghamshire.

Superficially the Vale of Trent landscape can appear uneventful while, in places, industry and urban development erode any sense of rural tranquility or picturesqueness. Major roads including the A1 and A17 hurry across the land unsympathetically and the growing settlements of Grantham, North Hykeham, Gainsborough and Scunthorpe all sit within the Vale. The Trent power stations at Cottam and West Burton are a dominating presence in the northern Vale, adding a dramatic focus to the landscape but also generating cloud and sulphurous trails. In spite of all this, though, the Vale has much of interest, including a varied and distinctive landscape that repays closer exploration.

The character of the Vale is complex and enigmatic, being intermediate between a typical Midland clay vale and the more open flatlands of

FACING PAGE: **River Trent at Newton Cliff**

RIGHT: **Vale of Trent sunset, Lincoln**

94

Lincolnshire. However, these two states are intermixed closely rather than being fully blended, giving a constantly changing landscape that is hard to pin down initially. Thus, areas of hedged fields with oaky lanes, fox coverts and old pastures occur alongside more open, fen-like country with occasional stands of poplars and fewer hedges. Tracts of forest and heathland add further to the landscape mix.

This variety reflects the Vale's geology. The bedrock itself is divided between Mercia Mudstone to the west and Liassic clays to the east. The boundary between the two lies just east of the River Trent and is marked in places by a low scarp, seen most clearly at Trent Cliff near the Humber. Superimposed on this basic pattern are a variety of much younger drift deposits which form the land surface across large areas.

Lincolnshire shares the Vale of Trent with Nottinghamshire and the area has various landscape features often associated with the latter county including oak trees and compact villages of red brick and pantile. Hedgerow oaks are more common here than elsewhere in Lincolnshire and are the predominant tree in some parts of the Vale, due probably to the influence of estates such as Doddington, Burton and Belvoir. Conversely, the Vale's spectacular skies and wide expanses clearly align it to the rest of Lincolnshire. In places the landscape is reminiscent of Belgium or the Netherlands and the cultural influence of the Low Countries contributes an intriguing layer to the Vale's history, architecture and character.

FACING PAGE: **poplar stand, Coleby Low Fields**

TOP RIGHT: **hedgerow oaks near Doddington**

RIGHT: **cottage near Aubourn**

The Liassic clays are exposed mainly in the lower-lying areas crossed by the Rivers Witham, Brant and Till and have a farmed landscape dominated today by arable cropping. The rivers are heavily embanked but previously fed floodplains and wetlands such as Aubourn Fen, Bassingham Fen and Burton Fen. These wetlands had been reclaimed by the 19th century though, ironically, several areas of farmland near Lincoln are now used as washlands to protect the city from flooding. The valleys have large arable fields punctuated by poplar stands and small woods, with occasional pastures surviving as a reminder of the mixed farming that typified the Vale's claylands up to the post-War decades.

Glacial tills east of Gainsborough resemble the clay vale, but other drift deposits give markedly different landscapes. Sands and gravels left by rivers and glaciers form a belt of country east of the Trent Valley between Newark and Scunthorpe, with a spur reaching to Lincoln via Eagle and Doddington. Here also are patches of windblown Coversands that were deposited as inland dune systems after the last Ice Age. Soils in this belt are mostly light and infertile and formerly supported heathland and rabbit warrens. Specialist crops like turf are a feature of the sandy soils today.

Lincolnshire's share of the Mercia Mudstone country is minor and largely covered by drift deposits but has distinctive pinky-red soils that, where exposed, are strongly redolent of Nottinghamshire and the Triassic Midlands. Curiously, the modern Trent does not enter the Liassic vale and sticks instead to Triassic rocks all the way to the Humber. This was not always so, however, as the river flowed east through the Lincoln Gap at least once during the last Ice Age, leaving behind the extensive river gravels

Sand and gravel deposits in the Vale of Trent once supported extensive tracts of heathland. Breeding birds recorded historically in these areas include great bustard, ruff, dunlin, stone curlew, Weller's sandgrouse and black grouse. Sadly, most of this heathland and its wildlife have been lost over the last two hundred years due to reclamation, industry and afforestation. The Agricultural Revolution of the 18th and 19th centuries saw the less acidic 'commons' and 'moors' enclosed using 'corn and sheep' farming to improve soil fertility. Folding sheep on the Vale's light gravel soils continues today, as here **near Bassingham** (ABOVE). The more acidic heaths and warrens of the Coversands generally survived longer but have been extensively damaged or destroyed by urban growth, sand extraction, cessation of grazing and planting with conifers.

Laughton Forest (LEFT & ABOVE) was created from the 1920s on a large expanse of sandy heathland and bog called Scotton Common, dramatically changing the area's ecology though retaining fragments of heath, wetland and pools which are now managed for nature conservation. Black grouse disappeared from the area in the 1940s, but its fauna now includes woodlark, nightjar, crossbill and adder.

The River Trent is not renowned for its beauty and the river's lower reaches in Lincolnshire are perhaps the least regarded of its entire course from the Staffordshire moors to the Humber. Clusters of pylons, industry, artifical banks and the river's feint but distinctive chemical smell make it easily dismissed when compared to rivers such as the Thames or Severn. However, the lower Trent Valley has a surprisingly varied landscape that is worth exploring for its wildlife, history and walking. The valley is at its most picturesque where wooded bluffs adjoin the river, as at Newton and Knaith, while Trent Cliff adds unexpected drama to the landscape near Trent Falls. Other parts of the valley are flatter and more open and have correspondingly big skies. The Trent itself has many moods according to season, weather, flow and tide. The river also changes with age, becoming wider and more obviously tidal as it approaches its confluence with the Ouse to form the Humber.

ABOVE: **sunset over the River Trent from Trent Cliff**

LEFT: **Wildsworth village beside the River Trent**

which are quarried west of Lincoln, and may originally have followed a course further south through the Ancaster Gap.

The Trent Valley itself is a distinct corridor landscape within the wider Vale. Over millennia the river's changing course and frequent flooding have created a broad alluvial floodplain with wetlands called 'marshes' that were used seasonally for grazing by the Trentside villages. Today the river is tightly contained by floodbanks and the former marshes have largely been drained and ploughed on the Lincolnshire bank. Low bluffs bound the floodplain on the east and the Mercia Mudstone occasionally creates more prominent features as at Newton Cliff and Gainsborough.

Historically the River Trent has been a major physical barrier whilst also providing one of Lincolnshire's main routes to the outside world. Even today bridges are few and far between, but the river's trade has dwindled almost to nothing and survives mainly as memories in the Trentside villages and Gainsborough's regenerated waterfront. The Trent is tidal as far as Cromwell Lock (Notts) and has a tidal bore called the aegre or aegir.

The basic pattern described above – a clay-based vale set between the Trent Valley and the Lincoln Edge – is modified at the area's southern and northern extremities by ironstones, which have exerted a major influence on the landscape and its development. In the south, a rich orange-brown ironstone called marlstone increases in thickness and slews away from the

RIGHT: **River Trent at Burton-upon-Stather**

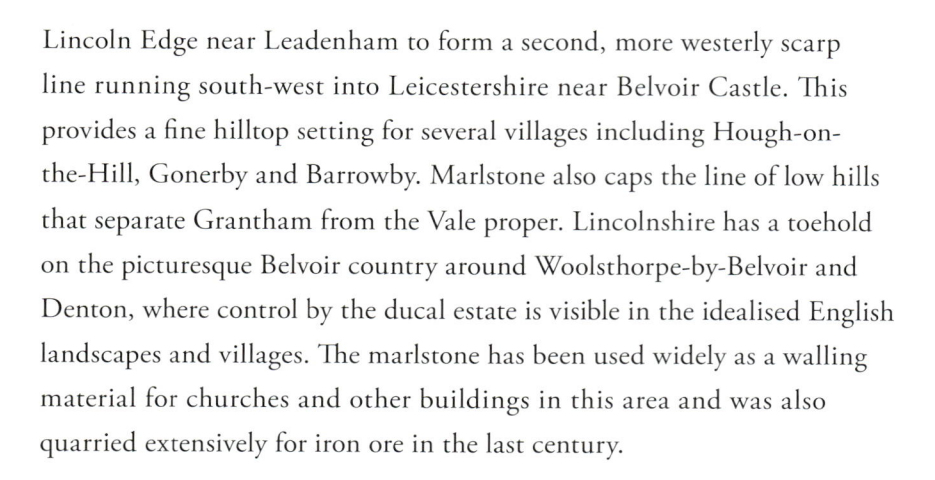

Lincoln Edge near Leadenham to form a second, more westerly scarp line running south-west into Leicestershire near Belvoir Castle. This provides a fine hilltop setting for several villages including Hough-on-the-Hill, Gonerby and Barrowby. Marlstone also caps the line of low hills that separate Grantham from the Vale proper. Lincolnshire has a toehold on the picturesque Belvoir country around Woolsthorpe-by-Belvoir and Denton, where control by the ducal estate is visible in the idealised English landscapes and villages. The marlstone has been used widely as a walling material for churches and other buildings in this area and was also quarried extensively for iron ore in the last century.

Beneath the Marlstone scarp the Vale of Trent blends southwards into the Vale of Belvoir near Bottesford. Before World War II this corner of Lincolnshire shared a countryside of pastoral farming with the nearby Leicestershire hills and Vale of Belvoir, though this character has been weakened substantially by the widespread shift to arable.

At the opposite end of the Vale of Trent, around Scunthorpe, the Frodingham Ironstone creates another bench of higher ground between the Lincoln Cliff and the Trent. Scunthorpe's gargantuan steelworks and former ironstone workings dominate the landscape here, with more rural countryside occurring around Alkborough. The Frodingham Ironstone

TOP LEFT: **marlstone hills seen from the Lincoln Edge, Harlaxton**

TOP RIGHT: **marlstone walling with limestone details, Denton**

contains the iron ore that drove Scunthorpe's rapid industrial expansion as an iron and steel town from the 1860s and also contributes geologically to Trent Cliff, the striking scarp feature which overlooks the River Trent as it approaches its confluence with the Ouse at Trent Falls.

Early human settlement in the Vale is thought to have focused initially on the lighter soils near the Trent Valley, leading to the development of sophisticated enclosed landscapes for arable and pastoral farming by the Iron Age. Reclamation of the Vale's claylands probably commenced later but was also well advanced by this period.

The present-day settlement pattern of the Vale dates back to the village nucleation of the Anglo-Saxon period and strongly reflects the area's topography and natural resources. One line of villages follows the Lincoln Edge with its springs and access both to vale farmland and the grazing land of the adjoining limestone heaths. South of Lincoln these are sometimes known as the 'cliff villages'. A second, looser line of villages runs parallel to the first in mid-Vale from Scunthorpe to Saxilby, where it dissolves into a fuzzier pattern in the southern Vale. A third group of villages follows the Trent itself, these having a role historically in the river's trade and/or as ferry crossing points. Shrunken and deserted Medieval villages occur throughout but are most common on the heavy tills of the northern Vale.

RIGHT: **Claypole church**

The Vale shows both early and Parliamentary enclosure in its surviving field patterns. These embody a process of change over several centuries from the Medieval landscape of open fields, heaths and warrens to the present farmed landscape. As elsewhere in Lincolnshire, agricultural intensification in the post-War decades has eroded but not destroyed older patterns.

Away from the limestone and ironstone scarps, traditional domestic and farm buildings in the Vale are almost entirely of brick and red pantiles. The architectural influence of the Low Countries can sometimes be seen in the brickwork of older buildings, including 'tumbled-in' gables and occasional Dutch or shaped gables.

Churches in the Vale are typically more modest than those of the Fens and Kesteven Fen edge, though Brant Broughton and Claypole rank amongst the finest gothic architecture in Lincolnshire and the ancient minster church of Stow is a prominent landmark in the northern Vale.

LEFT: **willow tree in farmland near Scampton**

ABOVE: **sunset with stormclouds over the Trent Valley**

LEFT: **Doddington Hall**

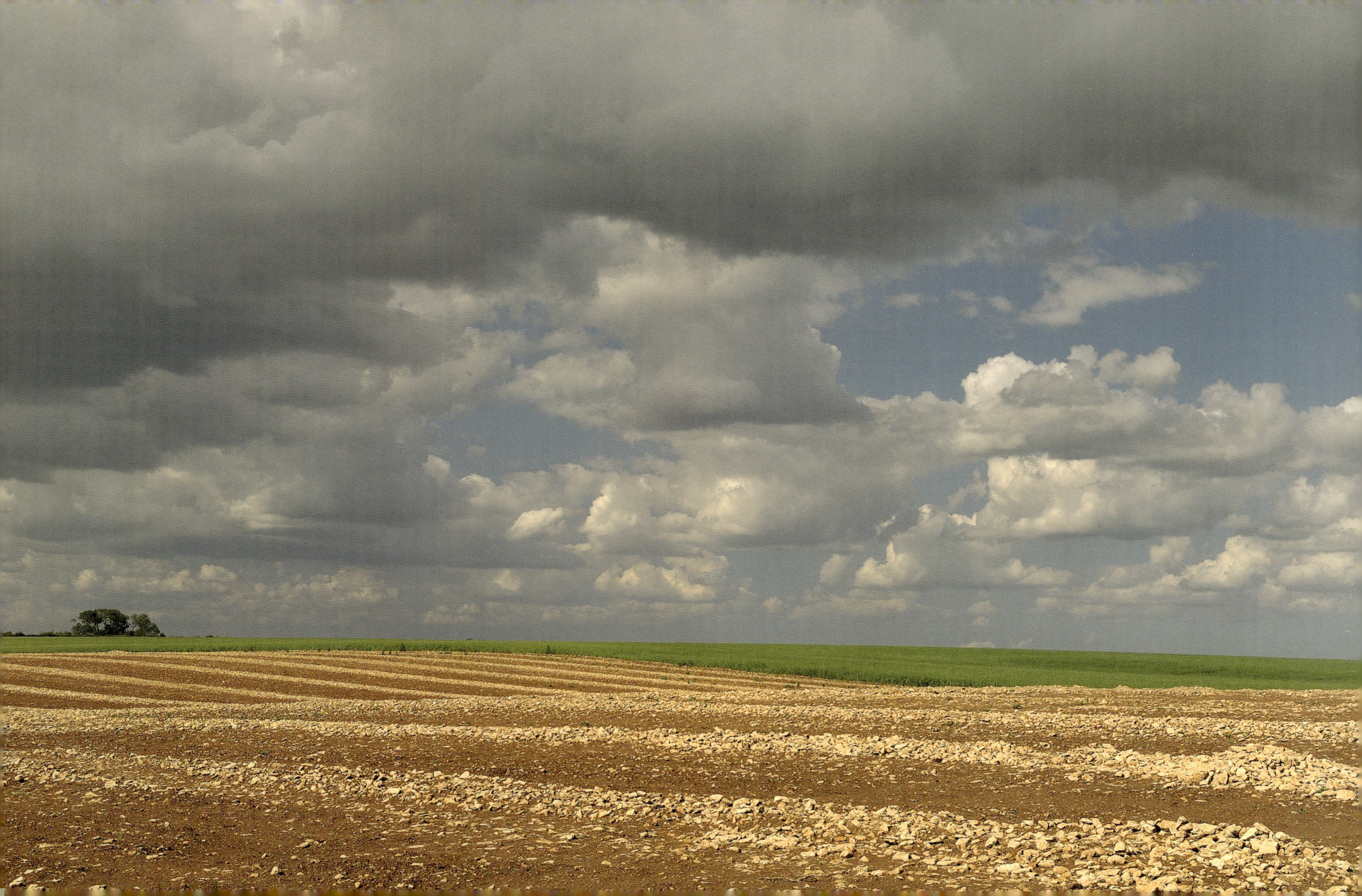

III - HEATH & CLIFF

Jurassic limestones form a belt running the entire length of Lincolnshire from Stamford to the River Humber. This is part of the so-called Stone Belt of England which also includes the Cotswold hills and the limestone uplands of Northamptonshire and Rutland. Within Lincolnshire the belt has shared qualities throughout, including a dry plateau landscape, reddish-brown soils and attractive stone architecture. However, it is divided into three sections by 'gaps' where east-flowing rivers have carved through the limestone, and each section also has its own individual identity.

Between Stamford and the Ancaster Gap, the limestone plateau is often cut by valleys and has extensive Ice Age deposits, producing the varied and well-wooded countryside of the Kesteven Uplands (see Chapter IV). North of Ancaster the plateau narrows gradually into a single ridge that runs due north to the Humber and has a more open and elemental quality. The section from Ancaster to the Lincoln Gap is called the Lincoln Heath, often shortened to the Heath, while north of Lincoln the whole ridge is known locally as the Lincoln Cliff or simply the Cliff.

Both the Heath and the Cliff are uplands in Lincolnshire terms due to their elevation above the adjoining flatlands. However, the height of the land is modest, reaching a maximum of just 372 ft (114m) at Normanton Heath. The Cliff is lower still and only rarely exceeds 200 ft (61m). The relief of both areas is similarly subdued and forms an open plateau of gentle undulations and shallow valleys that are dry in their upper part. The drama of these uplands lies in their sweeping expanses and wide skies rather than sudden contours, though the western margin of the plateau is an exception where the Lincoln Edge forms an escarpment overlooking the Vale of Trent.

The Lincoln Edge signals the geological structure of both the Heath and the Cliff, which is a tilted ridge or 'cuesta'. Behind its steep western scarp

FACING PAGE: **limestone rubble in field, North Carlton Cliff**

RIGHT: **roadside pines, Blankney Heath**

the limestone plateau dips gently eastwards and sinks ultimately below the clay bedrock of the Fens and Mid Lindsey Vale. This structure is due to the past uplifting and tilting of Lincolnshire's sedimentary rocks, coupled with the limestone's greater resistance to erosion compared with the adjoining clays. The Lincoln Edge and most of the plateau are formed from Lincolnshire Limestone, the best-known of the county's Jurassic limestone formations and its finest building stone, while younger limestones including the Great Oolite and Cornbrash outcrop on the plateau's eastern margin.

East of the limestone plateau a band of Fen edge country separates the Heath from the Fens proper. This has a mixed geology of Jurassic clay, glacial till and river gravels, and a correspondingly varied landscape of

ABOVE: **Lincoln Edge seen from Coleby Low Fields**

RIGHT: **limestone field wall with lichen, Green Man Lane**

FACING PAGE: **Lincoln Edge, South Carlton**

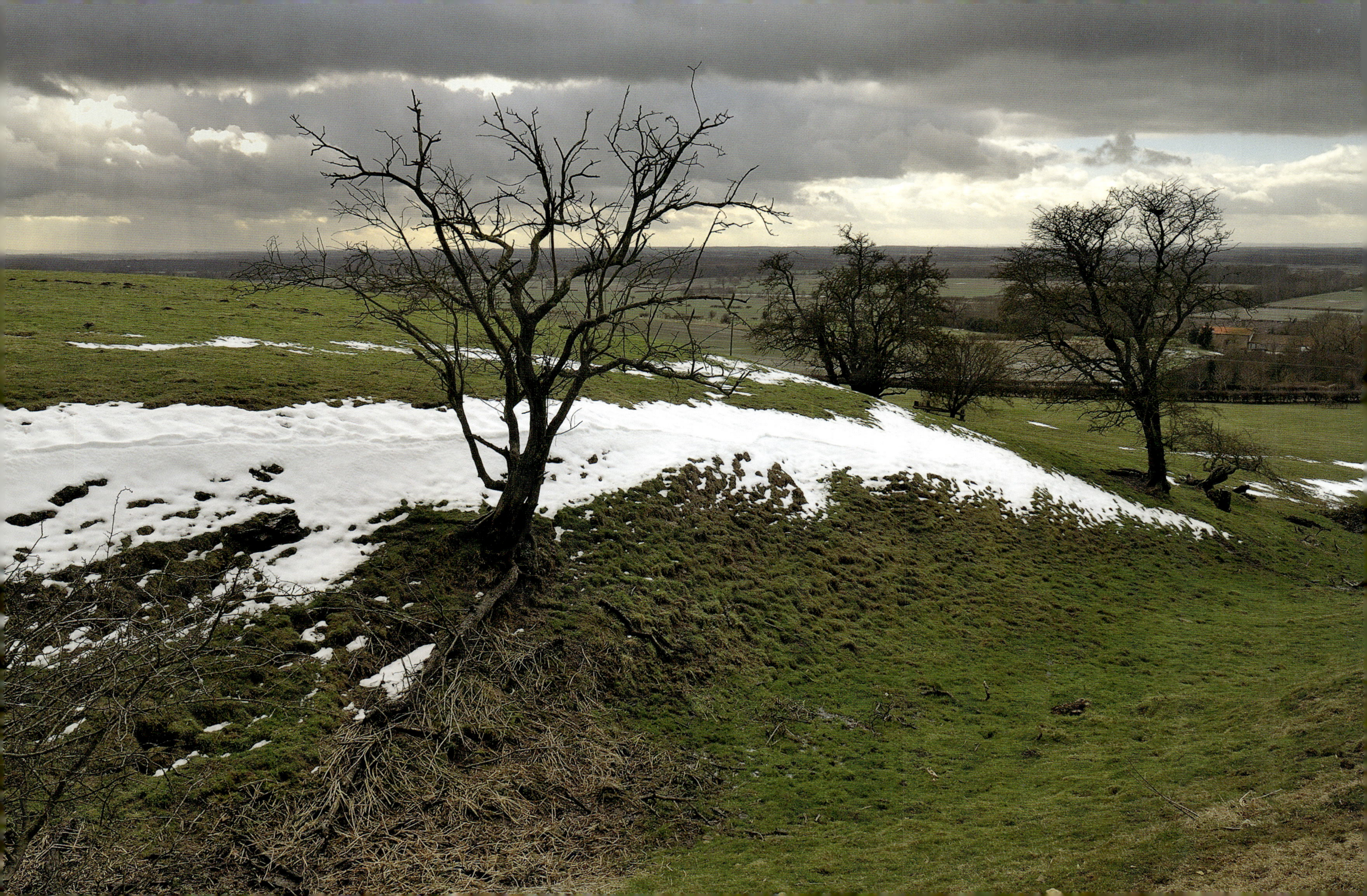

woods, former 'moors' and small hills called 'barffs' overlooking the flat fenland. North of Lincoln the Cliff plateau blends eastwards into the lowland clays and reclaimed carrs of the Mid Lindsey Vale.

As the plateau of the Heath and Cliff is virtually free from drift deposits, the soil rests directly on the limestones and is often strikingly rubbly when ploughed. The main exception occurs on the Cliff near Scunthorpe where Coversands have blown onto the limestone and created a localised landscape of sandy heaths and forestry plantations, as at Risby Warren.

Prior to its enclosure and conversion to arable in the late 18th and early 19th centuries much of the plateau was limestone 'heath'. The open, gorsy grasslands were used for centuries as rough grazing and rabbit warrens and may have dated back to the original clearance of woodland from the area by prehistoric farmers. The Lincoln Heath was so wild and extensive that a lighthouse was erected at Dunston between Lincoln and Sleaford to guide travellers in the mid 18th century. Enclosure brought new farmsteads to the plateau which was otherwise almost devoid of settlement until the RAF developments of the last century. Medieval settlement stuck to the margins

LEFT: **Dunston Pillar.** This land lighthouse beside the modern A15 was built in 1751 by Sir Francis Dashwood to assist travellers when the Lincoln Heath had a reputation as a desolate and even dangerous area. It was surmounted by a lantern that was regularly lit until the 1780s, when enclosure of the Heath and road improvements rendered it redundant. In 1810 a statue of George III replaced the lantern but this too was removed in World War II, when the tower was lowered in height to reduce the risk to aircraft using the airfield on Coleby Heath.

where springs gave rise to two parallel lines of villages along the Lincoln Edge and eastern fringe respectively. Each village had its share of limestone plateau for grazing and usually gave its name to its particular piece of Heath or Cliff. These parish-based subdivisions have endured as place names on the Heath today and form loose pairings such as Harmston Heath and Nocton Heath. A similar but less complete pattern survives on the Cliff plateau with Saxby Cliff, Owmby Cliff, Willoughton Cliff and so on.

Much of the present-day landscape dates back to the enclosure period, including the large fields and straight, wide-verged lanes. Typically the fields have neatly trimmed hedges or, particularly on the Heath, drystone walls in various states of decay. Hedgerow trees are mostly ash or beech. There is virtually no ancient woodland and the scattered woodland blocks and shelterbelts all postdate enclosure, emphasising how open the earlier heaths must have been. Almost nothing remains of the former heath vegetation, which is now confined to road verges and quarry margins.

Heather or limestone grassland? Place names such as Grange de Lings suggest that heather once grew locally on the limestone plateau. However, it is unclear whether it ever supported tracts of true heath vegetation on leached soils like the chalk heaths of East Anglia. Historical accounts and the remaining flora indicate that limestone grassland and scrub predominated prior to agricultural reclamation. Today, limestone verges have calcareous (lime-loving) species that were probably widespread on the grazed grasslands of the Heath and Cliff before enclosure.

TOP RIGHT: **limestone flora on High Dyke, Lincoln Heath**

RIGHT: **Small scabious (*Scabiosa columbaria*) beside Bloxholm Lane**

Enclosure of the heaths ushered in the era of 'corn and sheep' farming. As part of the new crop rotations of the Agricultural Revolution flocks of Lincoln Longwools were folded in the fields to strip graze on fodder crops such as turnips, thereby improving the light soils with manure. In the last century potatoes and other cash crops became more important but 'corn and sheep' farming continued into the post-War period. Today, folding is only occasionally seen and the plateau is almost exclusively arable. Alongside wheat, sugar beet and oilseed rape, the area retains its historical importance for malting barley and limestone-grown potatoes are still a speciality. More recent crops have included daffodils, gladioli, linseed and opium poppies for the pharmaceutical industry.

TOP LEFT: **hawthorns in winter, High Dyke, Harmston Heath**

BOTTOM LEFT: **limestone field wall, Temple High Grange**

The landscape of the Lincoln Heath prior to enclosure was dismissed by most 18th century writers as a "dreary waste", especially by agricultural improvers like Arthur Young who championed its reclamation. Today we can only imagine the natural beauty of the vast, grassy expanses and their lost ecology, which included great bustard and stone curlew. However, the Heath plateau is still amongst the best places to experience Lincolnshire's big skies and spectacular cloudscapes. The plateau is at its most dramatic and elemental when stormclouds cross the expanse of fields in the winter half of the year, as in this March scene on **Dunston Heath** (FACING PAGE). The area also retains interest for wildlife including hares and farmland birds such as skylark and lapwing.

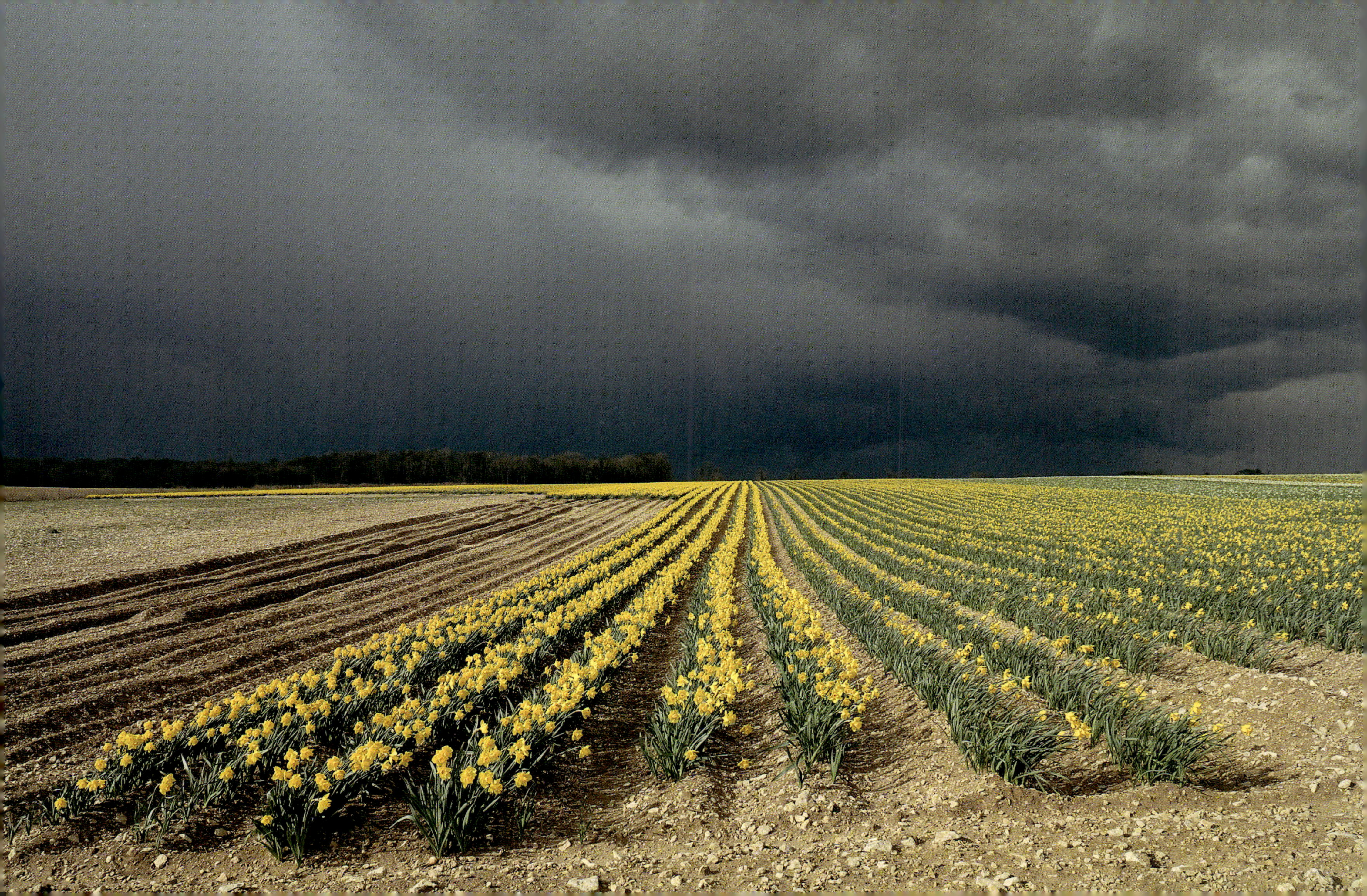

Both Heath and Cliff have a marked linear quality due to the narrowness and straightness of the limestone ridge. The main historic transport routes emphasise this north-south grain, particularly Ermine Street, which follows a classically straight Roman course close to the western edge of the plateau from Ancaster to the Humber. South of Lincoln it is called High Dyke and is today made up of a series of minor roads and green lanes suitable for walkers. North of the city it carries the modern A15 as far as Scawby, then a quieter B class road to Winteringham. An earlier, prehistoric route known as the 'Jurassic Way' is thought to run along the crest of the Lincoln Edge and bears the name Middle Street north of Lincoln.

So far the shared characteristics of the Heath and Cliff landscape have been emphasised, but they also have subtle differences. The Heath plateau is generally broader and feels less completely tamed by agriculture, as if something of its past as a wilderness and haunt of outlaws has never been completely dispelled. Comparatively, the Cliff is a narrow and elevated ridge from which views outwards are more prominent, and has an airier

LEFT: **beech tree in winter, Dunston Heath Lane**

OPPOSITE PAGE: The Cliff plateau is open and expansive even by Lincolnshire standards and offers wide views towards the distant Wolds when conditions are clear. It is characterised by large and sweeping arable fields yet trees, hedges and coverts nevertheless provide focus and intimacy to the landscape. These views of the Cliff are at **Welton Cliff** (TOP), **Spridlington Cliff** (BOTTOM LEFT) and **Burton Cliff** (BOTTOM RIGHT).

113

though slightly aloof feel. Even more than the Heath it is now a landscape of agri-business, although several country house estates and their parklands make a significant local contribution to landscape character, including Riseholme, Hackthorn, Fillingham Castle and Norton Place.

As well as creating breaks in the Lincoln Edge, the river gaps are distinct from the plateau as landscapes. Both were cut by rivers larger than those of today. The Lincoln Gap is now used by the River Witham but was probably enlarged by the Trent when the latter was diverted during the Ice Age. Later it became the dramatic setting for the city of Lincoln with its Roman core and wonderful Medieval cathedral. The winding Ancaster Gap is less certain in origin but may represent an even earlier course of the Trent or an early Witham. Despite containing the famous Ancaster Stone quarries, it is essentially rural in character. Lastly, the Humber marks the northern termination of the Cliff at Winteringham, which has wide views across the river to Yorkshire. Geologically this is also a gap as the Jurassic limestones re-appear briefly north of the Humber near North Cave.

Prehistoric use of the limestone plateau is difficult to establish, as intensive arable farming over the past two centuries has eroded much of the area's archaeology through ploughing. However, crop marks have survived that show ditched enclosures dividing up the plateau both north and south of Lincoln, probably related to Iron Age farming. It is unclear whether these were territorial boundaries and/or for controlling livestock, or even if the plateau was mainly arable or pastoral at this date. Iron Age settlements

ABOVE: **Coleby church.** Coleby is one of a series of villages along the Lincoln Edge south of Lincoln, sometimes referred to confusingly as the Cliff villages.

FACING PAGE: **Lincoln Edge near Waddington.** The modern Viking Way long distance footpath runs along the crest of the Lincoln Edge as it approaches Lincoln from the south, here following the probable route of the prehistoric 'Jurassic Way'.

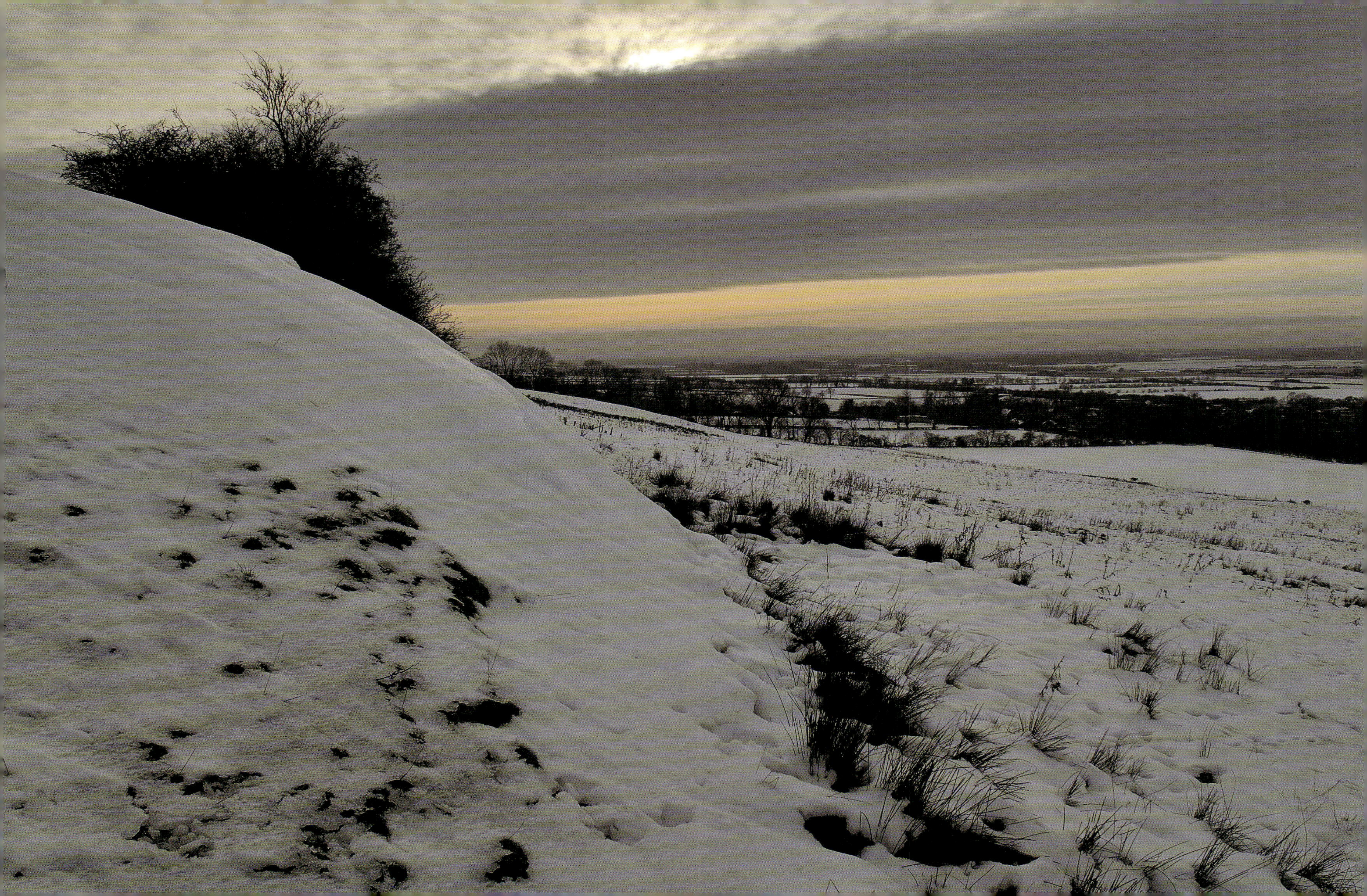

116

The Fen edge is a distinct landscape zone up to several miles wide lying between the Heath plateau and the fens of the Witham valley. A line of village settlement follows the zone between Lincoln and Sleaford, having been established in early Medieval times to exploit the spring line and access to both Heath and Fens for grazing and other resources. Earlier, prehistoric settlement had also located here for similar reasons. Sometimes the need to oversee fen grazing led to daughter settlements that may have been seasonal initially, such as Branston Booths and Potterhanworth Booths. The belt has varied clay and gravel soils that support woodland in places, but the former 'moors' (probably rough vegetation on sour soils) have largely been reclaimed for arable use. A similar zone occurs along the eastern margin of the Cliff plateau.

FACING PAGE: **Witham Fens from Metheringham Barff**

ABOVE LEFT: **Blankney**

ABOVE RIGHT: **Nocton Wood**

have been identified on the Cliff, including Dragonby, and these were augmented in Romano-British times by towns and villas, as well as the Roman military centre at Lindum (Lincoln) which later became a civilian city. Some time after the Roman departure, most of the plateau seems to have become the uninhabited heath of grassland and warrens that lasted until Parliamentary enclosure.

Limestone is the main construction material for almost all types of traditional building on and adjoining the plateau, including churches, villages and farmsteads. Additionally, ironstone is found adjoining the limestone beds in places along the Lincoln Edge, where it too has been quarried historically as a building stone and for iron ore. The Greetwell area adjoining Lincoln has a complex history of ironstone mining and limestone quarrying during the last two centuries and may also have been exploited earlier by the Romans.

LEFT: **Temple Bruer.** The interior of the Lincoln Heath was virtually uninhabited between the Roman period and the Parliamentary enclosures but Temple Bruer was a significant exception. Here the Knights Templar developed a large farmed estate from the 12th century, focused on a preceptory church and village. A single tower from the preceptory is the most obvious survival today but other landscape features remain in the area including a network of green lanes which may have been established by the Templar estate for transporting wool and other produce.

ABOVE: **The Lincoln Gap.** Mist fills the Gap in this view from Lincoln's South Common on a December evening. The ridge of Jurassic limestone that forms the Heath and Cliff is breached here by the River Witham as it turns east towards the Fens. On the north side of the Gap, Lincoln Cathedral occupies a prominent hilltop location marking the start of the Cliff plateau and forming a landmark that is visible across large parts of Lincolnshire. The Lincoln Gap is thought to have originated approximately 2 million years ago with an eastward flowing river cutting through the limestone on a course from the Nottinghamshire hills to the North Sea. Later, the Gap was taken over by the Witham as this 'Lincoln River' was captured by the Trent to flow into the Humber. Geological evidence indicates that the Gap was further enlarged by Trent waters on at least two subsequent occasions during the Pleistocene (Ice Age), when the course of the lower Trent became blocked by ice sheets. The most recent such episode was in the final or Devensian glaciation some 50,000 years ago.

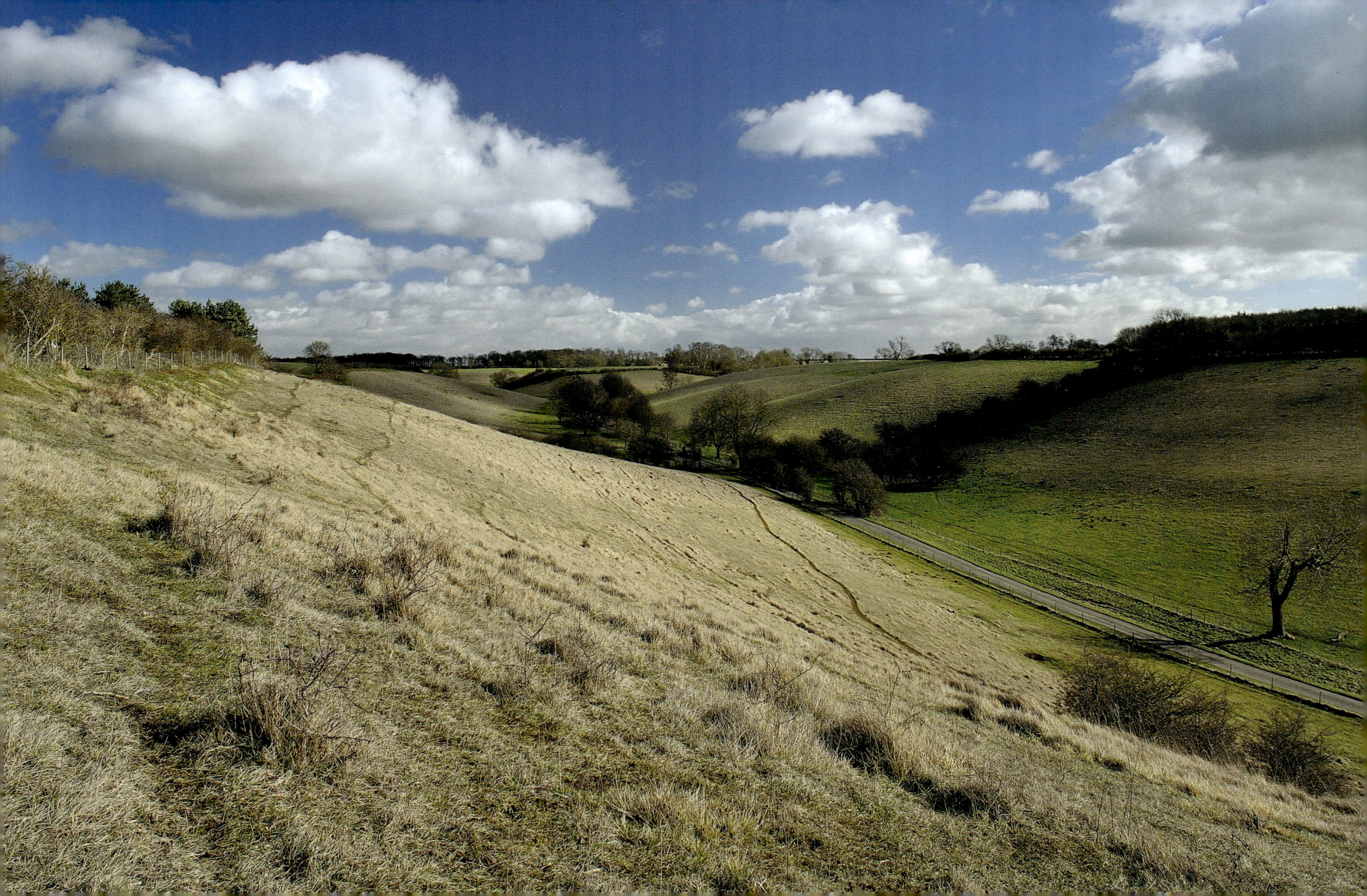

IV - KESTEVEN UPLANDS

The Kesteven Uplands occupy the south-western corner of Lincolnshire and form the southern portion of the county's Jurassic limestone belt as described in the previous chapter. In elevation they are only slightly lower than the Lincolnshire Wolds and reach almost 500 ft (152m) on the high border with Leicestershire. When seen from the Fens around Spalding, the Uplands clearly justify their name, rising abruptly on the horizon like a distant range of hills across the sea of fenland. Up close, though, the area is more plateau than hill country and mostly lacks the steep contours and airy ridges of the Wolds. Instead it is a gently undulating countryside of quiet charm where the valleys of the upper Witham and the twin Glen rivers have cut into the limestone plateau to create one of Lincolnshire's cosiest landscapes. Here are winding lanes, old pastures, attractive stone-built villages, country houses in landscaped parks and a feeling of settled continuity that is rare elsewhere in Lincolnshire.

The area is one of the most wooded in Lincolnshire, which adds further to its appeal for many people. Ancient woodland is widely scattered east of the Witham valley and the sylvan theme is augmented by the timbered parklands and estate planting of the area's numerous country houses. The association with woodland is long established as the Medieval Forest of Kesteven was centred on Bourne and included the adjoining plateau woodlands as part of its royal hunting territory. The name Kesteven itself is thought to mean 'meeting place in the woods', with an Anglo-Scandinavian provenance, and probably embodies the older Celtic element 'coed' (wood). It is possible that some woodland may never have been cleared and therefore have a continuous ecological lineage back to the native wildwood.

The Kesteven Uplands are defined by natural boundaries on all sides except the south-west where the plateau continues unbroken into Leicestershire and Rutland. The Ancaster Gap divides the area from the expanse of the

FACING PAGE: **limestone valley, Little Ponton**

RIGHT: **limestone cottages and headstones, Carlby**

122

Ancient woods and trees are one of the natural glories of the Kesteven Uplands. The area is particularly notable for old oak trees which have survived from the Medieval period. **The Bowthorpe Oak** (RIGHT) is over 1,000 years and has a girth of 42 ft (13m), making it one of the oldest and largest oaks in Europe. It is thought to have originated in a deer park that was subsequently converted to farmland. More ancient oaks survive nearby in **Grimsthorpe Park** (BELOW RIGHT) – these predate the initial creation of the parkland from a Medieval Forest landscape of scattered trees, wood-pasture and woodland. Even today parts of the Park retain the appearance of this earlier landscape. Management of the Uplands' woodland for hunting probably commenced with selective clearance by hunter-gatherers in the Mesolithic period. Clearance intensified as Neolithic and Bronze Age farmers created grasslands for grazing livestock.

FACING PAGE: **Tortoiseshell Wood**

Lincoln Heath to the north, while its western limit is marked by the escarpment of the Lincolnshire Limestone. The latter is a geological continuation of the Lincoln Edge but is more wooded here than further north. At their southern end the Kesteven Uplands decline gently towards the Welland valley and Stamford, where Lincolnshire meets the limestone country of Northamptonshire and Peterborough. Lastly, the long eastern margin of the Uplands drops to the Fens and is marked by a line of Fen edge villages between Sleaford and the Deepings.

The Kesteven Uplands have the same basic structure seen in Lincolnshire's other uplands, with a steep western scarp (here partly in Leicestershire and Rutland) and a plateau declining eastwards. However, the angle or dip of the rock strata is less here and the plateau is consequently far wider. In contrast to the sweeping linearity of the Heath and Cliff, this is a landscape that fills its own horizons and only offers distant views of other areas from its margins. The plateau thus absorbs the traveller and has a meandering, unhurried quality not unlike parts of Norfolk and Suffolk.

The bedrock of the Kesteven Uplands is entirely of Jurassic age, with the dominant limestones giving way to Oxford Clay on the eastern margin. Unlike the Heath and Cliff, however, Ice Age clays or tills cover the bedrock over wide areas. This greater variety of surface geology, coupled with the incised nature of the plateau, distinguishes the Kesteven Uplands topographically from the limestone belt further north.

In broad terms four main landscape types therefore make up the area – limestone plateau, river valleys, clay plateau and Fen edge – though these are not entirely discrete and intermesh in complex patterns. Limestone plateau occurs mainly in the north and west, where the Lincolnshire Limestone and similar limestones lie at the surface. The characteristic landscape here is 'heath' which despite its name has been entirely converted to agriculture. As on the Lincoln Heath, reclamation of the scrubby, open

LEFT: **limestone plateau near Wyville**

FACING PAGE: **West Glen valley at dawn**

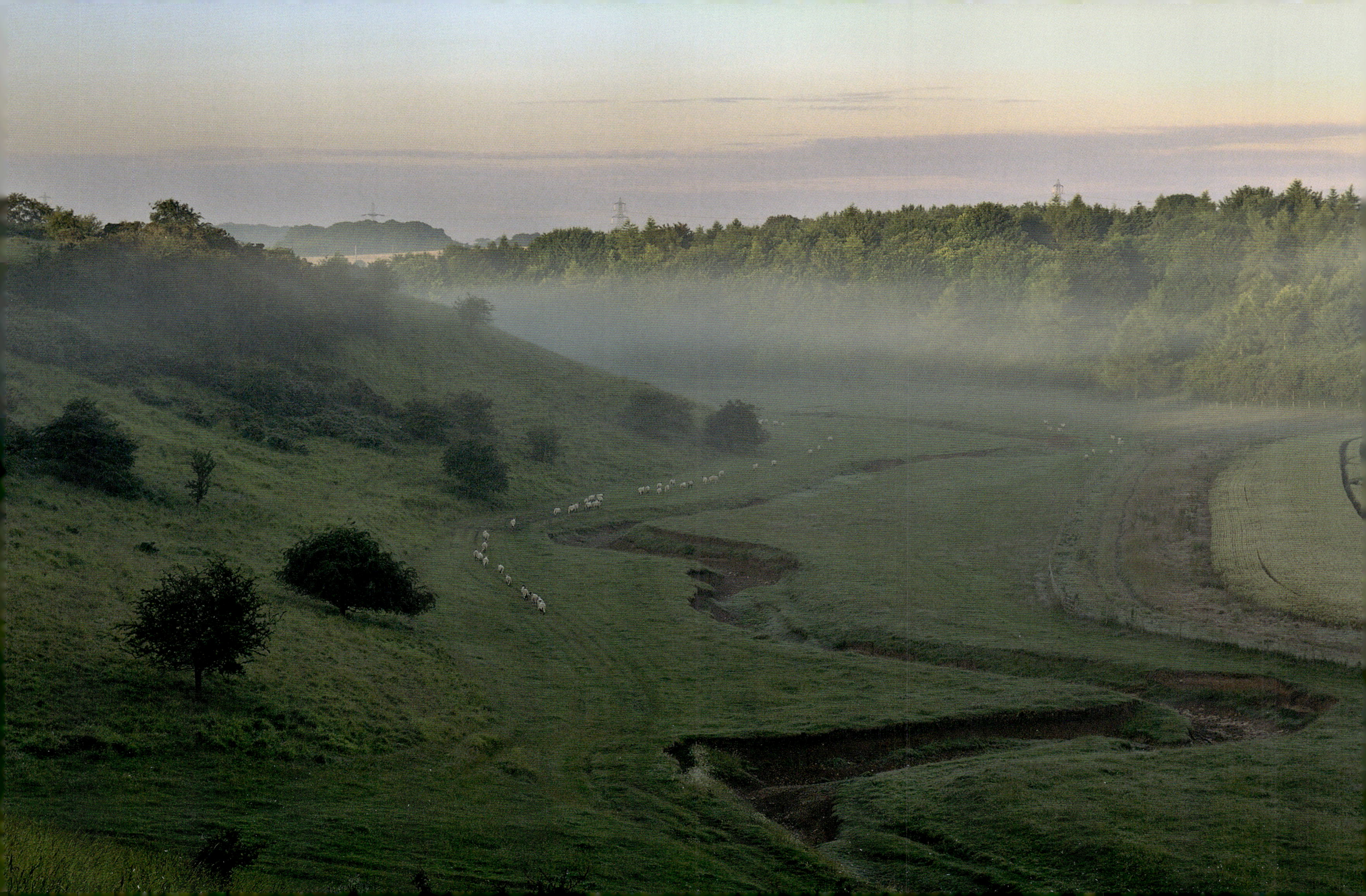

grasslands and warrens occurred mainly through Parliamentary enclosure and introduced a new regime of 'corn and sheep' farming that lasted for two centuries. These southern heaths form a continuous band adjoining the Ancaster Gap and along the western scarp. Today, the landscape shares many characteristics with the Heath and Cliff in being a wide, arable plateau of large fields and scattered farmsteads though it is softer and boskier in character, especially west of the Witham valley. The latter part of the plateau also has much more extensive outcrops of ironstone along the scarp which were heavily quarried for ore in the last century between Colsterworth and Buckminster (Leics) and near Harlaxton. This has left some unattractive scarring and areas where the surface has been lowered.

East and south of the heaths the countryside is more broken and rolling, where the valleys and tributaries of the Witham and the West and East Glen rivers have cut into the plateau. Limestone still forms the surface in places, especially along the valleys, but is only occasionally revealed on the plateau itself as at Swinstead. The valleys present an intimate and attractive landscape, especially where they have steep slopes of limestone grassland as at Swayfield and Woodnook. The broken terrain provides the setting for some of Lincolnshire's most picturesque villages, including Castle Bytham, Edenham and Creeton, and has been harnessed as natural landscaping

ABOVE RIGHT: **Temple Wood**

RIGHT: **cottage, Castle Bytham**

FACING PAGE: **Bassingthorpe**

127

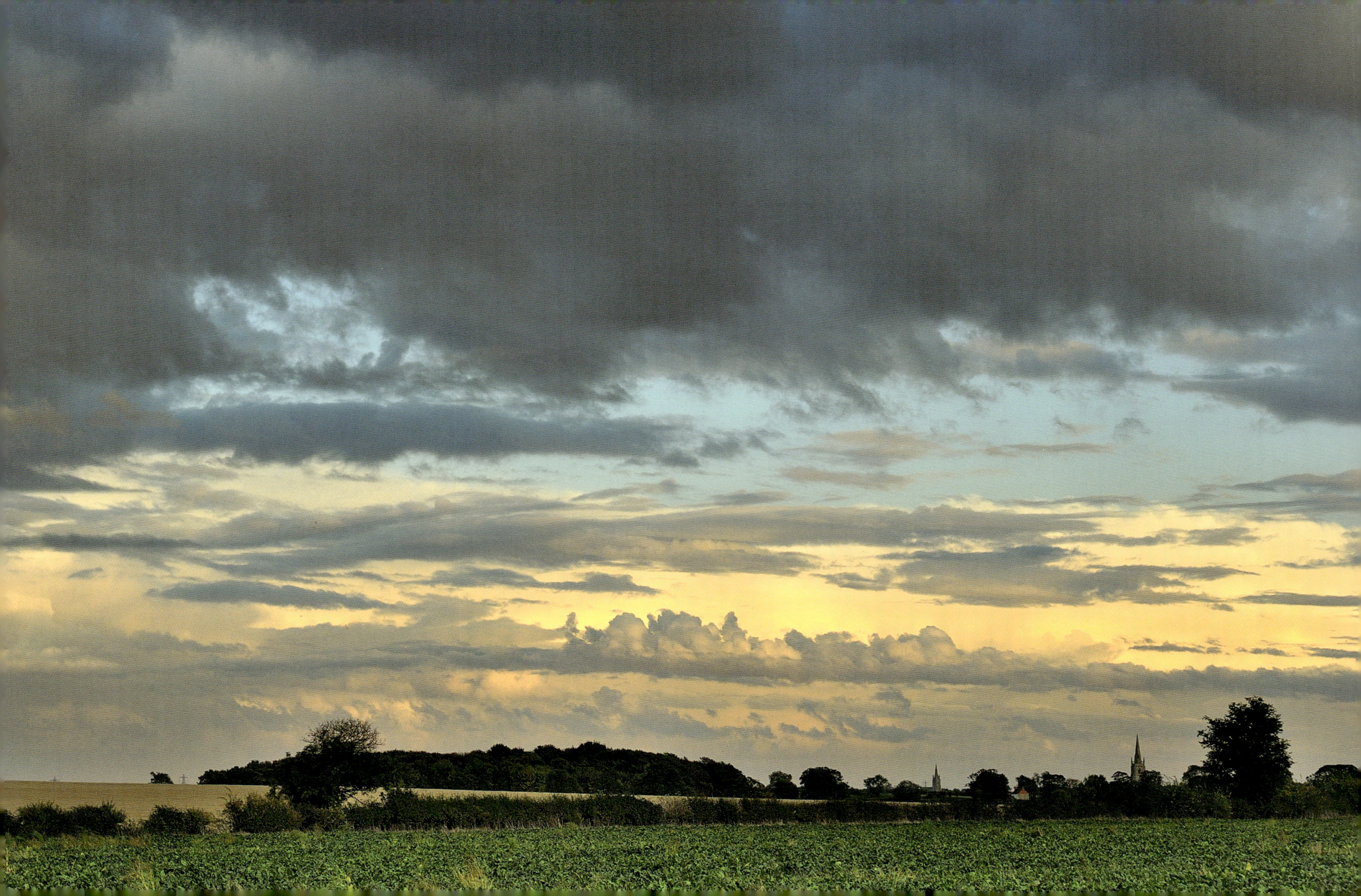

for country house estates including Grimsthorpe, Stoke Rochford and Holywell. Between the valleys the high plateau is capped extensively by till and has a clayey, wide but treed character with numerous woods as well as farmland. The clay soils favoured the mixed farming of wheat and cattle found on the eastern side of the Uplands for most of the last century though this has since lost ground to arable as elsewhere.

The easternmost part of the plateau from the East Glen to the Fens is a broad ridge of Oxford Clay capped by till and has only minor exposures of limestone. The landscape here is a far cry from the limestone heaths of the north and west, being dominated by clay farmlands, oaky lanes and ancient woods that once formed part of Kesteven's Medieval hunting forest. The final descent to the Fens is much gentler than the western scarp, but the ridge provides extensive views across the Fen edge and beyond.

The Fen edge is the transition zone where the Kesteven Uplands meet the Fens. As further north towards Lincoln, it is marked by a line of Medieval villages that exploited the combination of upland and wetland resources available. Towards Sleaford and Heckington the Fen edge becomes wider as the Uplands lose their distinct eastern edge and decline more gradually to the Fens. The geology of this area is complex, but tills dominate the large expanse of flattish country between the Slea valley and Horbling, slightly raised above the Fens, with Heckington at its centre. The term 'upland'

FACING PAGE: **Heckington and Asgarby spires from Kirkby-la-Thorpe**

RIGHT: **Ewerby church in the Kesteven Fen edge**

ABOVE: **Lincoln Red cattle on pasture near Irnham**

FACING PAGE: **The Drift near Skillington**. This prehistoric track crosses the lonely upland watershed between the Witham and the Trent and forms the boundary between Lincolnshire and Leicestershire. It probably originated in the Bronze Age and continued as an important transport route until later Medieval times, when it lost out to the better-serviced Great North Road and became a quieter drove road. Today it is followed by the Viking Way long distance footpath. The highest section of the route traverses the Lincolnshire Limestone plateau, including the second highest point in Lincolnshire near Skillington at about 490 ft (150m). The Drift is designated as a SSSI for its limestone flora but has been damaged by off-roading and tipping in recent years. New restrictions on vehicles will hopefully prevent further erosion. The Drift is also known locally as Sewstern Lane.

here is only a relative one that distinguishes the land from the adjoining fenland. However, the subtle undulations help to create a quintessentially Lincolnshire landscape in which the cornfields and occasional woods are punctuated by the spires and towers of numerous fine churches including Ewerby, Asgarby, Helpringham and, grandest of all, Heckington itself.

The varied natural environment of the Kesteven Uplands has attracted a human presence since at least Mesolithic times, with management of the landscape for hunting and agriculture evolving through the Neolithic and beyond. Early farming probably focused initially on the lighter limestone soils but the clays had also been cleared of woodland over large areas by the time of the Domesday Survey. The settlement pattern today essentially follows that which existed at Domesday though a number of Medieval villages have not survived. Except along the Fen edge, villages are scattered fairly regularly across the Uplands, with valleys and streams favoured as locations over the limestone heaths and clay plateau.

The Kesteven Uplands have examples of both early and Parliamentary enclosure. Parishes showing early enclosure form a block in the heart of the Uplands, possibly reflecting strong landowner control and/or their suitability for pastoral farming. By contrast most heath parishes remained unenclosed until the Agricultural Revolution of the late 18th century.

Limestone dominates the architecture of the area for all categories of traditional building including churches, farmsteads and houses of all

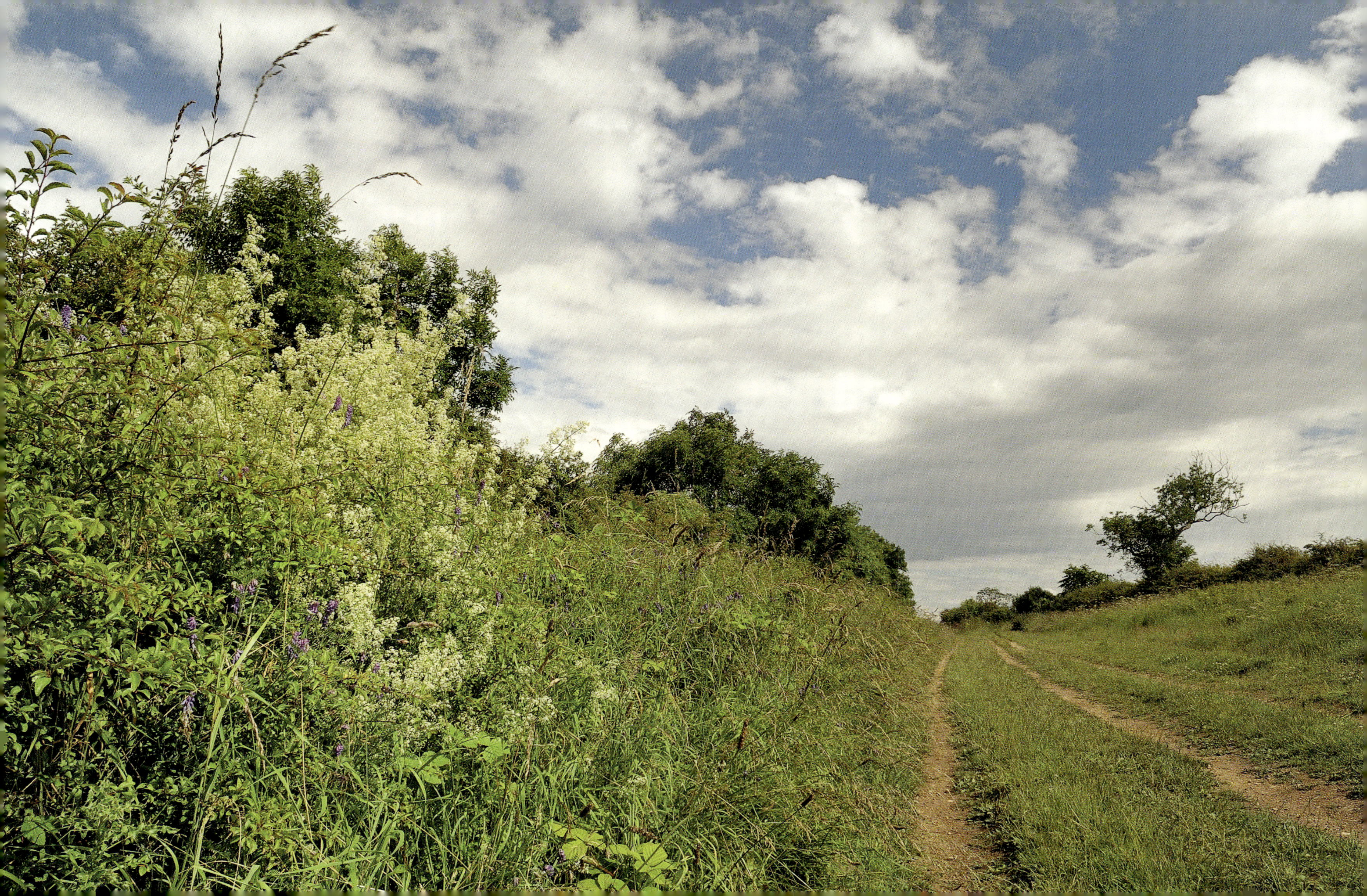

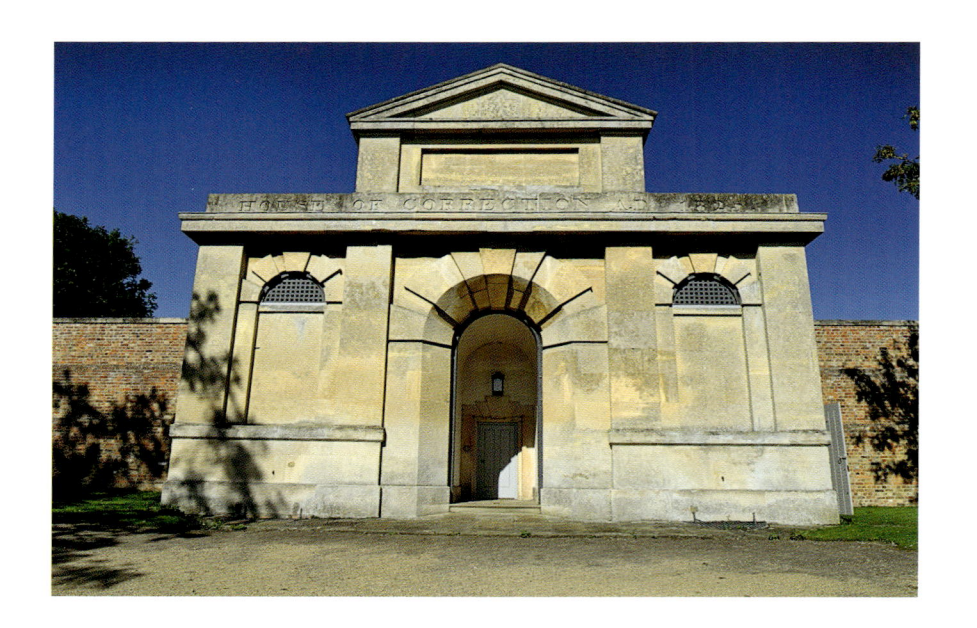

sizes and contributes greatly to its distinctive character, though building in brick is not uncommon. Roofing is generally of pantiles on vernacular buildings except in the south near Stamford where limestone 'slates' were imported from nearby Collyweston in Northamptonshire.

The area's magnificent churches, especially those of the Fen edge, have already been referred to and these are rivalled by a wealth of outstanding great houses. Within a few miles there are architectural exemplars of almost every period including Bassingthorpe, Belton, Boothby Pagnell, Culverthorpe, Grimsthorpe, Harlaxton and Irnham, amongst others. As noted previously, the landscaping and estate villages associated with these houses are a major influence on the landscape of the Kesteven Uplands.

TOP LEFT: **House of Correction, Folkingham**

LEFT: **Walled Gardens, Easton.** The existence of the walled garden is first recorded in 1592 when the manor of Easton was purchased by the Cholmeley family. Easton Hall was demolished in 1951 but the Easton estate is still managed by the Cholmeleys who are restoring the historic gardens as a visitor attraction.

FACING PAGE: **limestone architecture at Great Ponton**. The fine Medieval and Tudor architecture of the Kesteven Uplands reflects the wealth of its wool trade. Both the church tower and Flemish-style manor house at Great Ponton were built by a local wool merchant Anthony Ellys in the early 16th century.

133

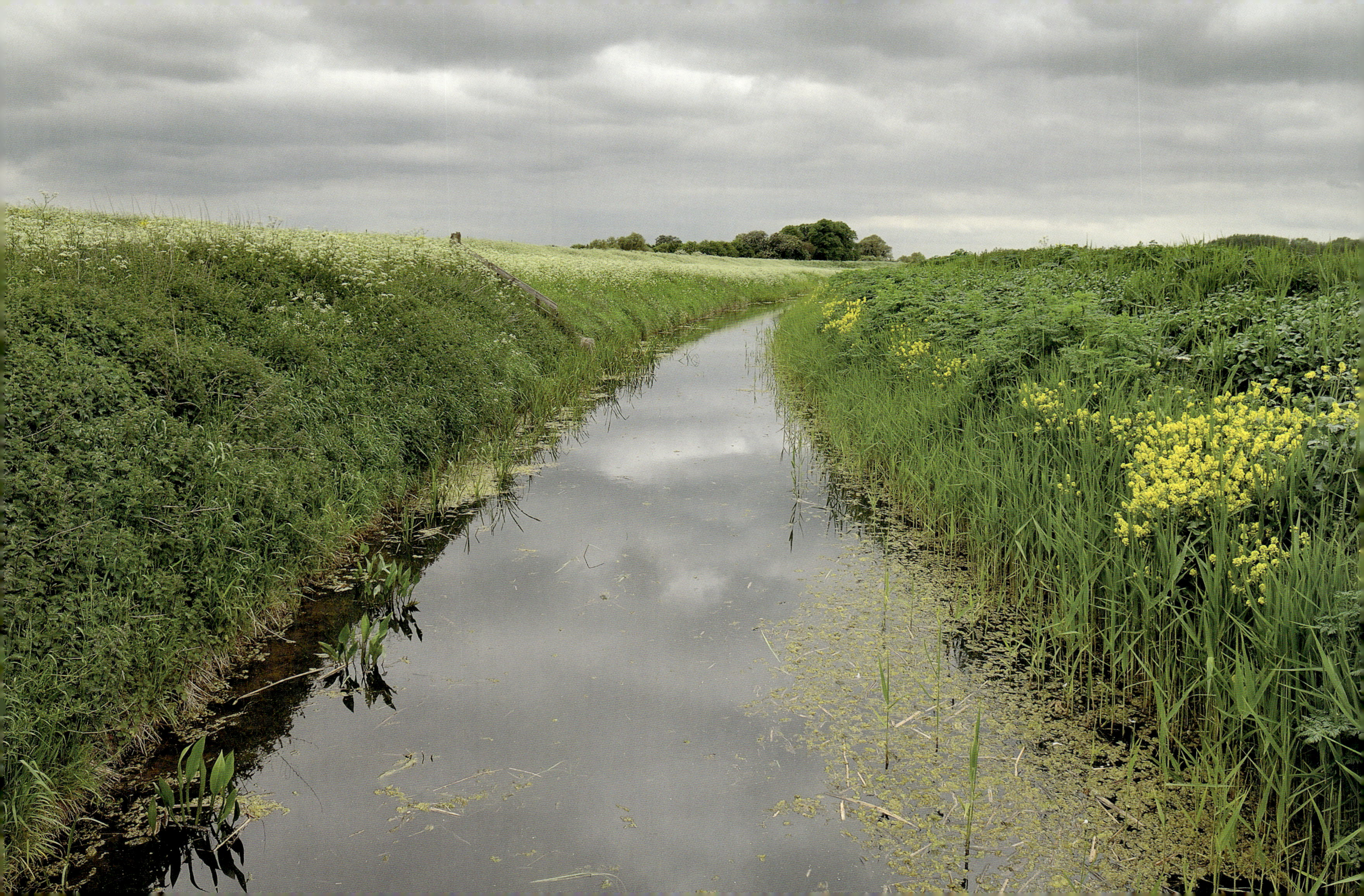

V - FENS & THE WASH

Most of Lincolnshire's lowlands once contained some freshwater wetland or fen, but one area has pre-eminence in taking its name from such – the Fens. Nowadays the term Fens or Fenland generally refers to the entire flat, low-lying basin around the Wash that reaches inland to Lincoln, Peterborough and Cambridge, and encompasses the reclaimed marshes and settled siltlands of the coast as well as the true fens of the basin's interior. This is by far the largest former wetland in England, stretching nearly 70 miles (112km) on its longest axis from north to south and up to 30 miles (48km) east to west. Prior to drainage it received the waters of four principal rivers – Witham, Welland, Nene and Great Ouse – which flowed tortuously seawards to the Wash and which still cross the area today in artificial channels controlled by sluices.

Lincolnshire shares the Fenland with a number of other counties, namely Cambridgeshire, Huntingdonshire, Norfolk and Suffolk, and the area as a whole has common threads of ecology, history and culture defining it as a distinct landscape entity. However, the Fens are far from being uniform throughout and also exhibit differences between south and north that offer a justification for this chapter's focus on the Lincolnshire portion. The south of Fenland was known historically as the Great Level and became the Bedford Level following Cornelius Vermuyden's drainage undertakings for the Earls of Bedford in the 17th century. It is an inland area lying mainly in Cambridgeshire and retains deep, dark peaty soils south of Peterborough and March in the aptly-named Black Fens, much of it below sea level due to peat shrinkage. Prior to drainage, its settlements were located mainly on islands in the fens, of which Ely is the largest and best known. North of the Bedford Level, the northern Fenland lies in Lincolnshire and Norfolk and, being mostly nearer to the sea, has more silt than peat at the surface and a coastal landscape of Medieval settlement and reclaimed saltmarsh arcing around the Wash. Its history of drainage is more incremental than that of the Bedford Level and was not completed until later.

FACING PAGE: **Fenland drain or 'lode', Welland Washes**

RIGHT: **River Nene approaching the Wash, Guy's Head**

Of all Lincolnshire's landscapes the Fenland is probably closest to the widespread image of the county as a flat and featureless expanse of arable farmland. To their detractors the Fens are variously monotonous, boring, bleak, depressing, even oppressive or menacing. Others, though, find the area compelling with its unique atmosphere and history. Flatness is certainly a defining characteristic of Fenland but if accepted can have a liberating quality with the ever receding horizons and 360 degree skies. In places the sense of space is awesome and occasionally almost North American. For the outsider there is also an intriguing foreignness in the landscape with its physical similarities to the Low Countries and the historic architectural and cultural links with the latter.

The flatness and strangeness of the Fens have encouraged myths and generalisations about their history. The familiar narrative is of a uniform arable plain created by the drainage of permanent swamps by Dutch engineers like Vermuyden, at which point the Fenlanders' traditional livelihood of wildfowling, fishing, reeds, peat and opium poppies was swept aside. This certainly holds true for some parts of the Fens, especially in the Bedford Level, but also obscures a more varied and complex picture. As explained below, the Lincolnshire Fenland contains a number of distinct but linked landscapes alongside the classic drained fen.

The Fen basin has evolved as a wetland over several millennia under the influence of both natural and human changes. Its development started in the Ice Age when ice sheets gouged the Jurassic clays that underpin the

LEFT: **Fen dweller and cottage in 2007, East Fen**

area and was shaped by the changes in sea level and climate that followed. An initial dry, wooded phase ended with the basin's gradual submergence by the sea from around 7,000 years ago, when advancing wetlands drowned the early forests. By 4,000 years ago, the Neolithic coastline reached inland to the upland margins and almost to Lincoln. Subsequently the sea retreated to its current position, but this happened unevenly and included at least two further marine incursions peaking in the Iron Age and post-Roman periods.

These environmental changes left the surface geology we see today. Marine conditions deposited the silts found in the seaward areas of the Fen basin, where former networks of tidal creeks can still be detected in the landscape as slightly raised banks called 'roddons'. Inland, freshwater swamp or fen conditions produced peat from the decomposition of vegetation. In the Lincolnshire Fens much of the surface peat has been lost by erosion and oxidation following drainage for arable farming, but pockets of peaty soil survive around Bourne and Crowland and in the Witham Fens.

Prehistorically, swamp prevailed across much of Fenland when the water table was high, particularly when rising sea levels reduced river gradients and marine silts impeded their access to the Wash. Ironically, early agriculture probably encouraged wetland formation through river silting as soils were washed from the newly deforested uplands surrounding the Fen basin during the Bronze Age. However, there were also periods when

TOP RIGHT: **reeds, willow and birch, Witham Fens**

RIGHT: **saltmarsh pool at sunrise, the Wash**

conditions were drier and allowed the expansion of settlement and farming. In Roman times, especially, a prosperous local economy of salt making and cattle rearing existed in the Lincolnshire Fens.

The marine incursion that followed the Roman period was a key event for Lincolnshire's Fenland. It not only buried much of the previous land surface beneath fertile silt deposits but also created a slightly raised ridge of land around the Wash that was sufficiently dry for permanent settlement to develop from early Anglo-Saxon times. This silt ridge lay along the Wash coastline of the time – then several miles inland from its current position – from Wainfleet to King's Lynn (Norfolk) and provided secure arable land as well as access to abundant grazing on the adjoining saltmarshes and fens. Known in Lincolnshire as the Townlands and in Norfolk as Marshland, the area had become one of the wealthiest and most densely populated parts of England by the 14th century with many fine churches.

During the Anglo-Saxon period the Townland communities began working together to build defensive banks for flood protection and reclamation of land for farming on both the seaward (marsh) and landward (fen) sides of the ridge and established daughter settlements on the new lands. Medieval

LEFT: **Gedney church**. Gedney is one of an arc of settlements originally established by Anglo-Saxon settlers on the Wash coastline. The modern village now lies several miles inland due to the reclamation of coastal marshland. The magnificent church is sometimes called the 'Cathedral of the Fens' and reflects the agricultural prosperity of the Townlands in Medieval times.

FACING PAGE: **saltmarsh creek, Gedney Drove End**

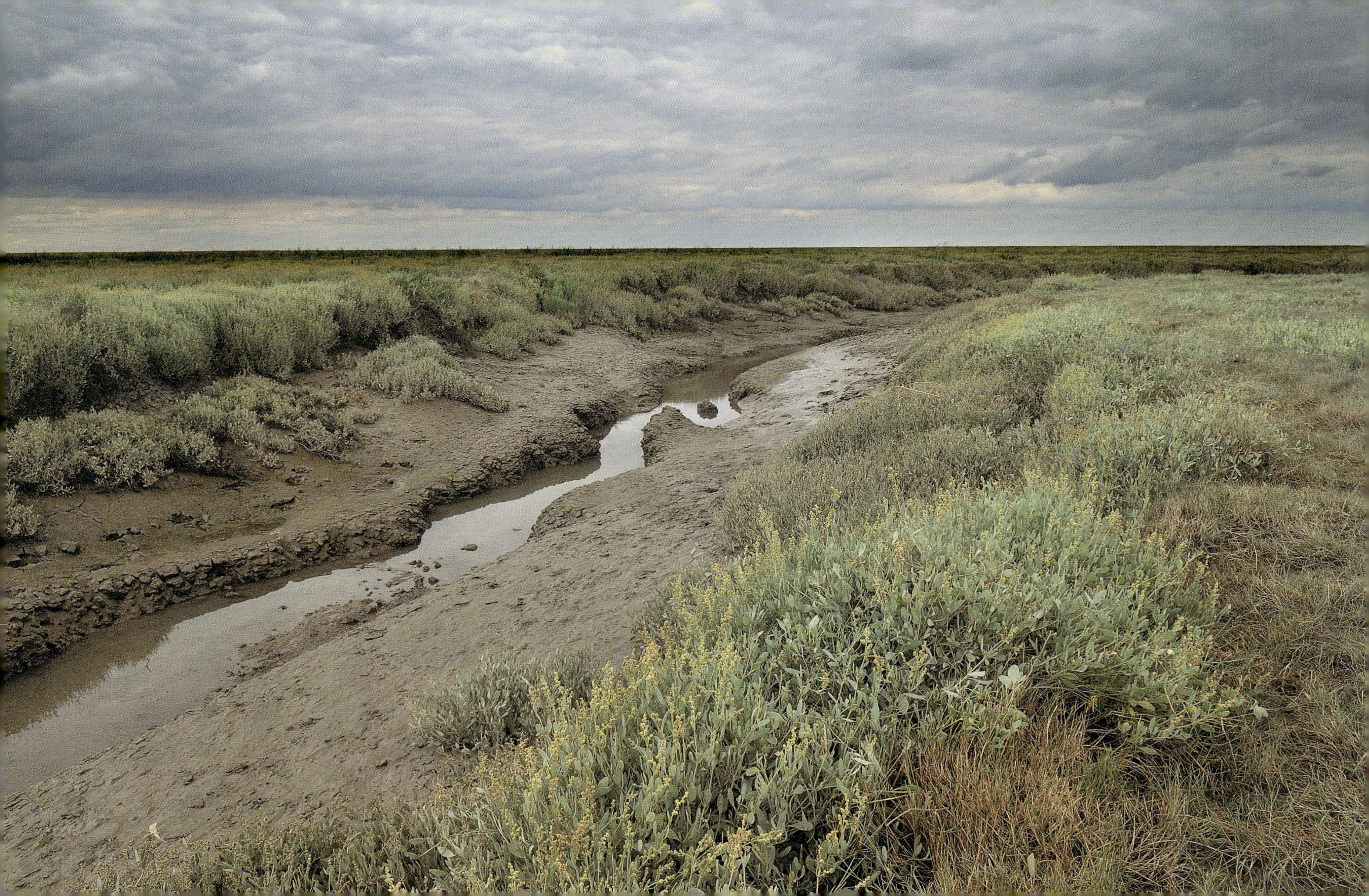

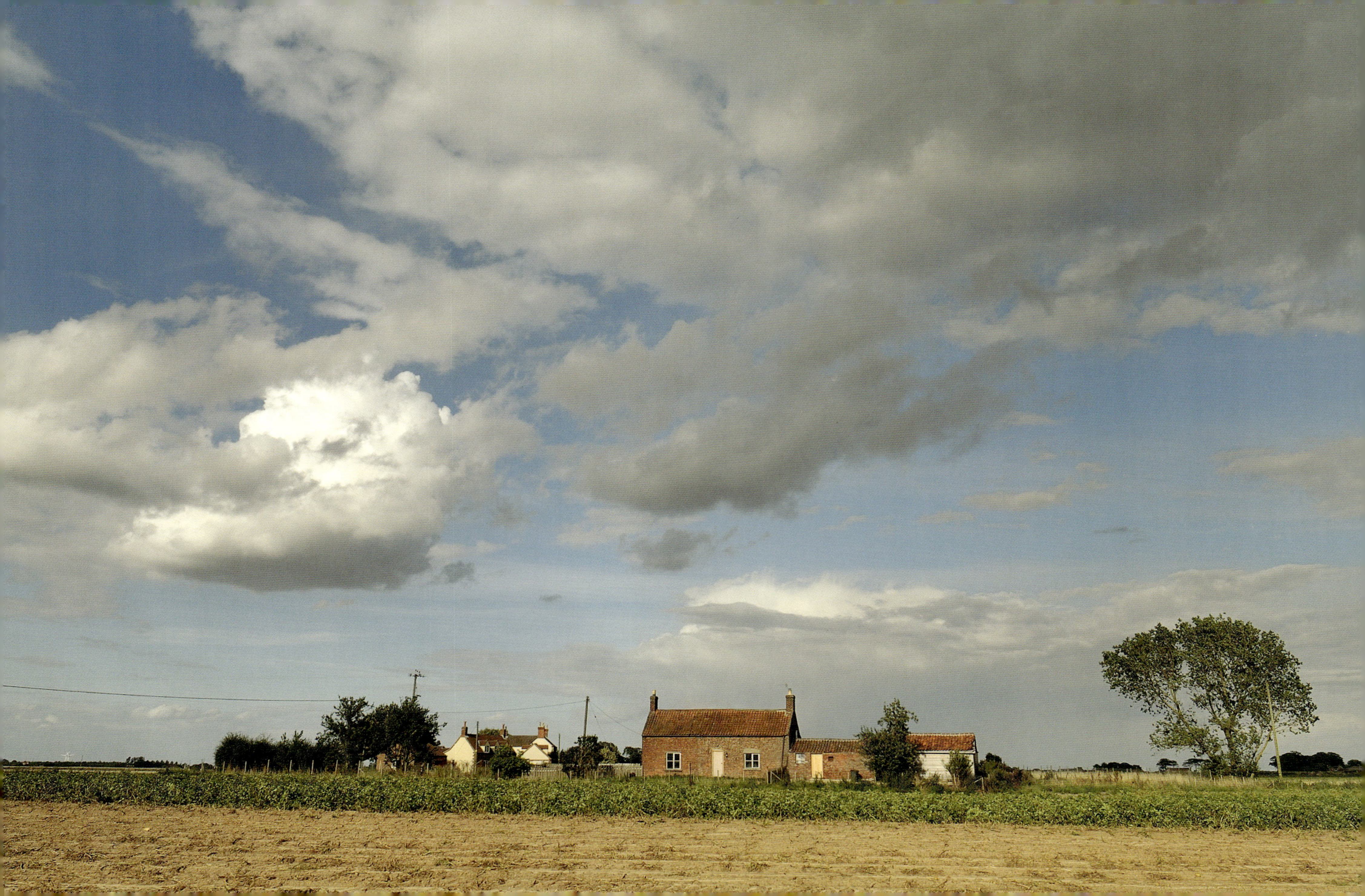

reclamation and enclosure was particularly extensive in the silt fens of Elloe south of the Wash. At the same time reclamation also occurred on a smaller scale from the Fen edges of Kesteven and the Wolds. Medieval reclamation nevertheless left a belt of wild fen between the Townlands and Fen edges, including Deeping Fen, Holland Fen, Wildmore Fen, West Fen and East Fen. A further spur pushed inland to Lincoln along the Witham valley. These wild fens were reclaimed and settled from the 17th century as part of large-scale drainage schemes, with the Wildmore, West and East Fens surviving into the 19th century. Prior to drainage they had little or no permanent settlement and were intercommoned by the surrounding villages for grazing, hay and other resources. Most lacked the meres found in the Cambridgeshire Fens before drainage, though the East Fen was an exception with its network of reedy pools or 'deeps'. Reclamation of saltmarsh also continued in the post-Medieval centuries up until the 1970s.

This complex history is manifest in the present-day Fen landscape, which has several distinct areas. The Townlands still stand out as the main area of

Modern agriculture has blurred but not erased the distinction between the Townlands and other parts of the Lincolnshire Fens. The Townlands landscape is more organic, intimate and populated and has Medieval origins that can still be traced in its churches, field patterns, lanes and other landscape features.

FACING PAGE: **dwellings, Friskney Eaudyke**

TOP RIGHT: **old enclosed pasture, Wrangle Low Ground**

BOTTOM RIGHT: **roadside poplar, Old Gate, Long Sutton**

settlement and contain all of the larger villages and towns. The landscape here is almost cosy by Fen standards, with a dense network of winding lanes, trees and farmsteads. Despite later changes, field and settlement patterns reflect the area's Medieval origins and growth, including the piecemeal reclamation of salt marsh and fen. The old Sea Bank shown on Ordnance Survey maps is an important survival that runs for miles across the landscape, marking the high tide line of the former Anglo-Saxon coastline. Remains of Medieval salterns form clusters along its route as it passes through previously coastal villages such as Holbeach Hurn and Surfleet Seas End.

Inland of the Townlands lie the Fens proper – the former freshwater wetlands that were seasonally or permanently wet before drainage. This is the classic Fen landscape of straight drains, straight roads and isolated farmsteads, though even here there is variation reflecting the long history of drainage. Areas reclaimed in Medieval times have some older settlements and churches, especially in the highly elongated parishes south of the Wash. Here, a succession of former fen banks and daughter settlements mark the progress of Medieval colonisation and numerous straight droves for

TOP LEFT: **Ruston Bucyrus dragline and drain, Dogdyke**

LEFT: **River Witham in flood near Five Mile Bridge, Witham Fens**. The Witham Fens between Lincoln and Chapel Hill were drained and enclosed under a series of Acts of Parliament from the late 18th century in connection with dredging and embanking work to the River Witham. Drainage channels or 'delphs' were constructed to carry water from the fens to the river, most of which are still in use today.

FACING PAGE: **storm passing over Moulton Fen**

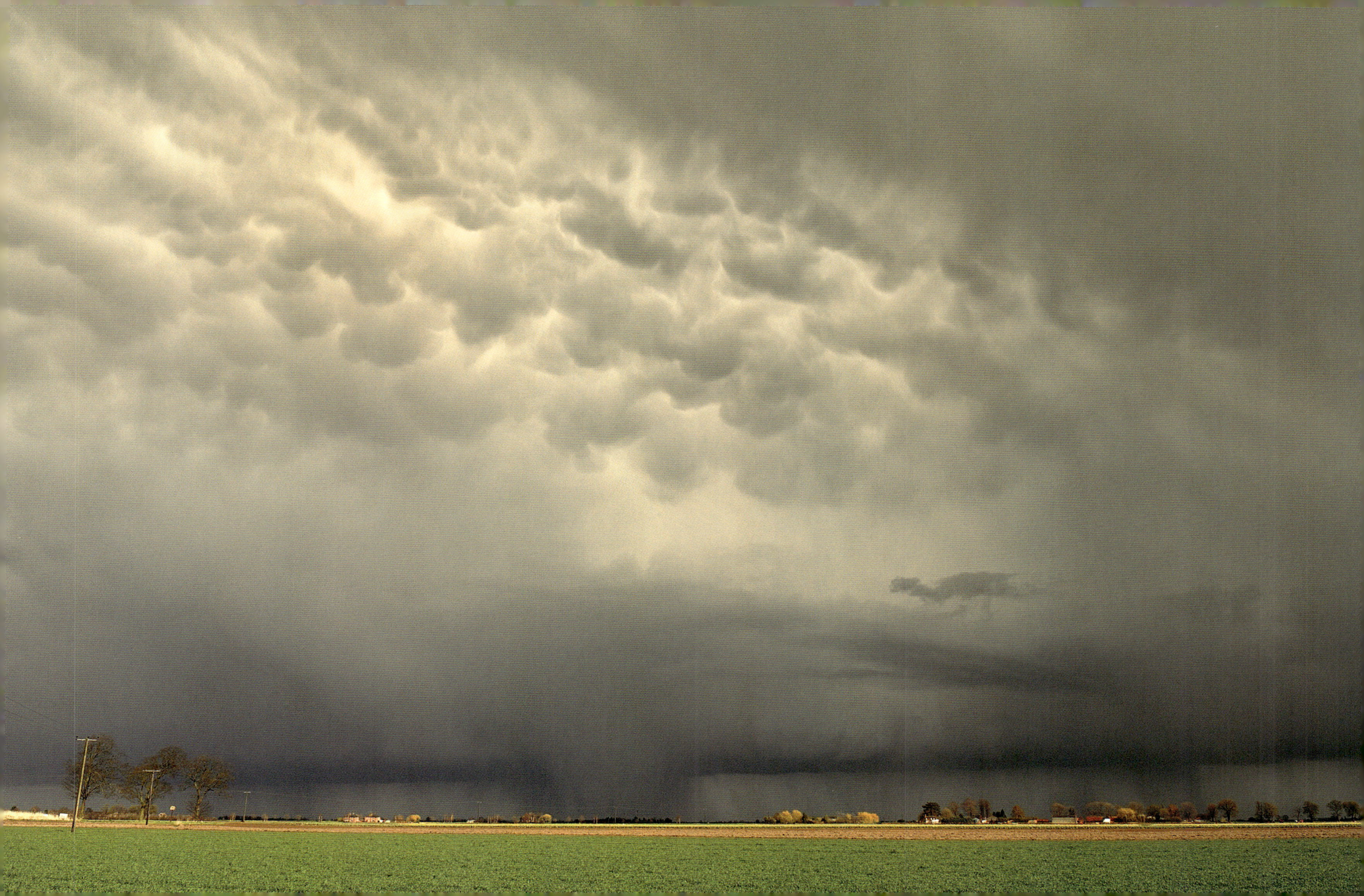

moving livestock survive as roads or tracks running for miles into the fens. By contrast the late-drained areas have virtually no older buildings and relatively few villages, though several new settlements were established in the 19th century including New Bolingbroke, Midville and Eastville.

Land reclaimed from coastal saltmarsh is the third main landscape of the Lincolnshire Fenland. It lies between the Townlands ridge and the present-day sea defences, forming a belt of varying width fringing the Wash. Though still referred to as marsh in place names it is now farmed intensively for arable and has little natural vegetation or grazing land. The landscape is superficially similar to the silt fens, with successive banks marking the reclamation of land from Medieval times, but is sparser and less rectilinear in appearance. In places it is surprisingly well treed, though it never entirely throws off its 'new' feel even in the older reclaimed areas. Under grey skies the area undeniably has a bleak quality but in fine

LEFT: **Crowland Abbey.** Lincolnshire has few fen 'islands' comparable to those of the Cambridgeshire Fens but Crowland is an exception that has provided dry land for settlement since at least the Roman period. The abbey was founded in the 10th century close to the site of the shrine of St. Guthlac, who had established a hermitage in the early 8th century. Crowland Abbey was involved in several drainage schemes in the Lincolnshire Fens up to the Dissolution, but Crowland remained as a seasonal 'island' until steam pumping was introduced in the surrounding fens in the 1800s.

FACING PAGE: **Counter Drain Washes.** These artificial washlands were created in the 1630s and 1640s to accommodate flood water from the River Glen. Most of the washlands were ploughed up in the 1950s but a small area at Baston Fen became a nature reserve and also hosts Fenland ice skating events when conditions allow.

145

weather its proximity to the sea gives a special brightness and clarity to the light and can sometimes heighten colours with a striking intensity.

Beyond the modern sea banks is the Wash. Despite military bombing ranges, this has large areas of natural landscape and internationally important bird populations. Salt marshes and muddy creeks provide the

ABOVE: **farmland and sea bank, Gedney Drove End**

FACING PAGE, TOP: **Lutton Marsh**

FACING PAGE, BOTTOM: **evening near Guy's Head**

foreground to expansive views that encompass shifting tides, sandbanks, mudflats and distant shorelines. It is a complete contrast to the intensively managed Fens and is perhaps Lincolnshire's finest wild landscape.

As noted above, patterns of settlement and enclosure in the Fens are linked intimately to the history of drainage and reclamation, with the Townlands and Elloe fens as the main areas of Medieval vintage. Irregular fields of early date surround the parent villages in the Townlands while the areas of Medieval reclamation often retain a simplified field pattern of narrow, ditched enclosures. In the post-Medieval areas, fields are generally larger though often still elongated and in blocks.

The draining of the Fens is well documented and often involved bitter conflict between different interest groups as seen in the Isle of Axholme. The Roman period saw the first major attempts at land drainage including the construction of the catchwater drain/canal called Car Dyke between Peterborough and Lincoln. Drainage improvements over the following centuries culminated in large-scale reclamation schemes from the 17th century onwards and the replacement of wind by steam power for pumping water in the 19th century. It was the latter that finally rendered all of Fenland reliably dry enough for commercial arable farming. In the last century steam pumping was replaced by diesel and then by electricity. With increasing freedom from flooding the Lincolnshire Fenland moved from being an area of national importance for cattle, sheep, horses and geese to highly productive cropland and has remained so ever since. The main

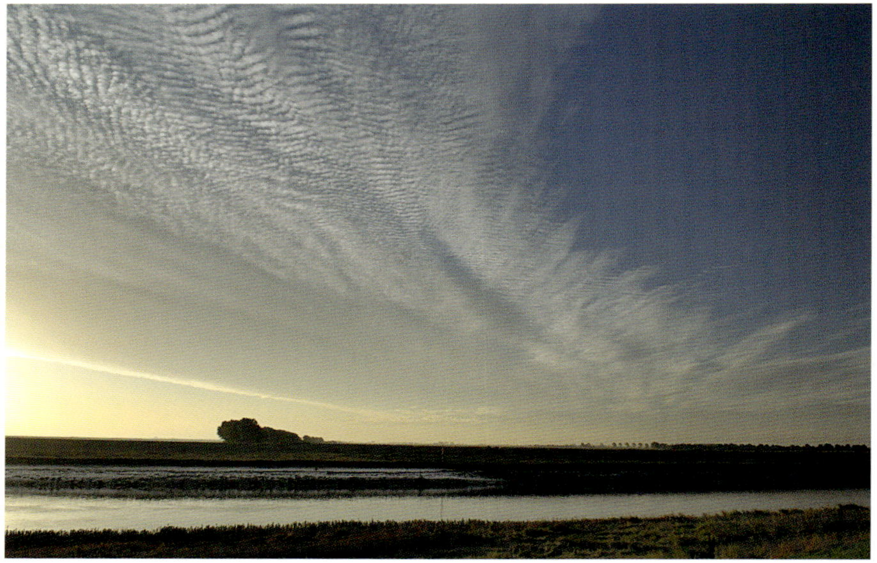

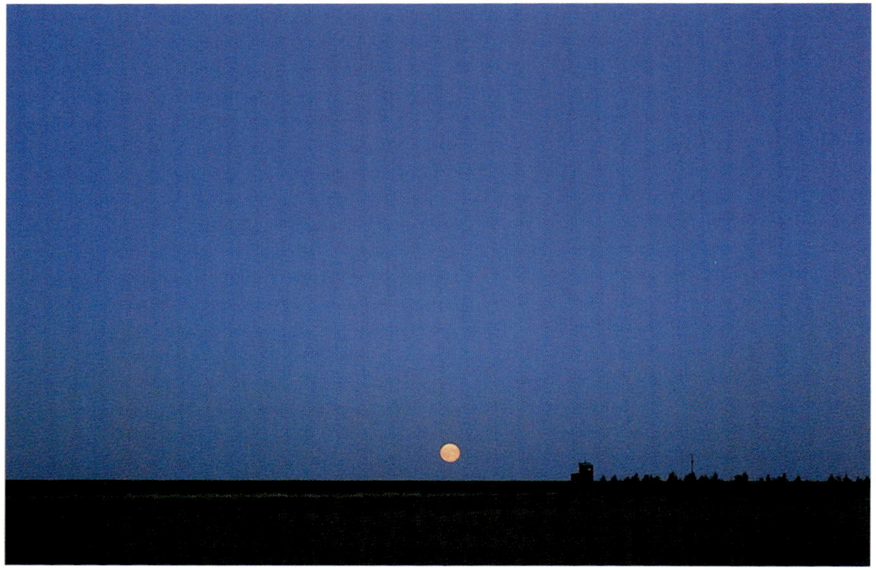

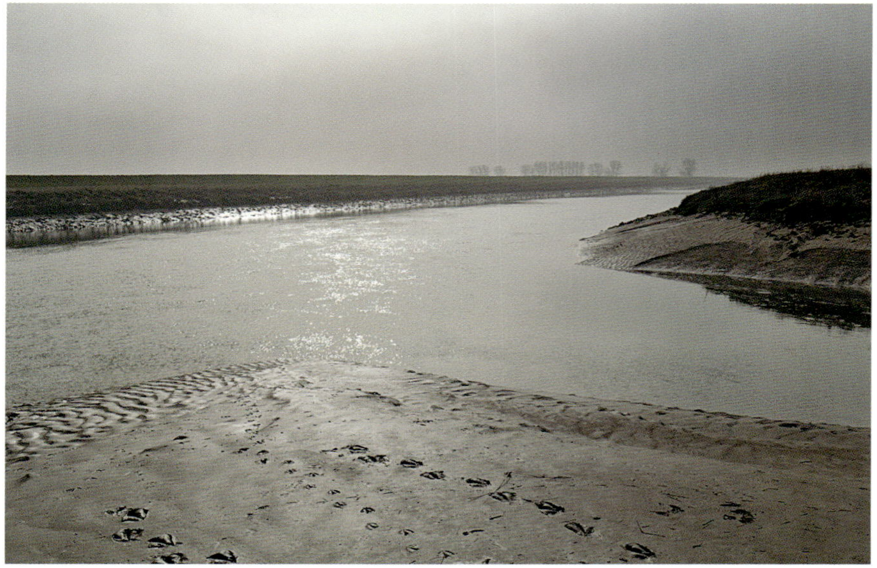

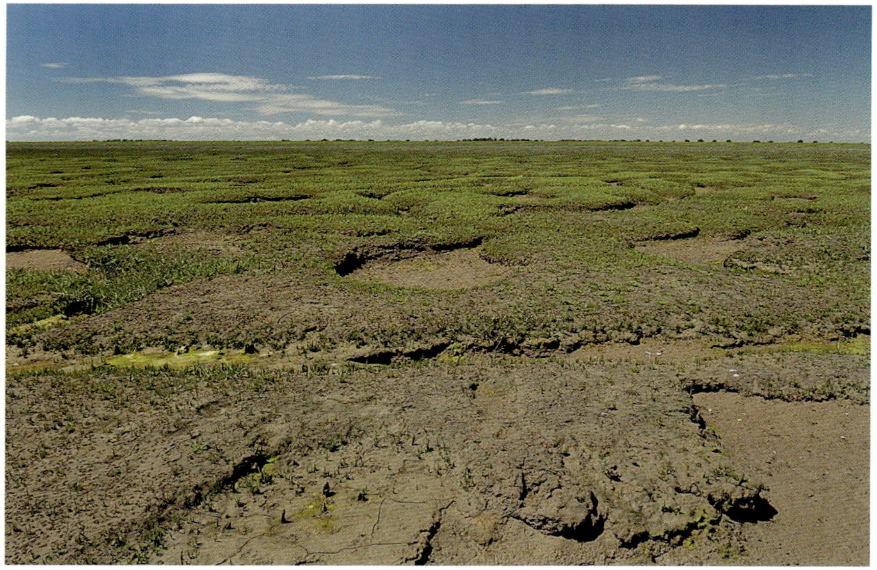

crops today are wheat, oilseed rape, root crops and vegetables, including potatoes, brassicas, leeks and onions. In the Spalding area the flower and bulb industry has been important since the 1890s.

The Medieval churches of the Townlands and the Kesteven Fen edge rank amongst the finest in the country, but most other types of building were either poorly represented in Fenland, such as country houses, or have not not survived well into the present century due to loss and renovation. Much of the area's vernacular architecture has been eroded in this way, though some traditional farmhouse and cottage building in brick and pantile can still be found, including examples of early brickwork showing Dutch influence. The characteristic 'traditional' Fenland cottage is detached with a catslide roof to the rear and is of 19th century date. Earlier cottage building in turf or mud and stud has vanished and even thatch is now rare. Preserved examples of pre-20th century architecture for drainage and pumping are uncommon but a fine working example of a steam engine house dated 1833 survives at Pinchbeck Marsh.

Landscapes of the Wash (FACING PAGE, CLOCKWISE FROM TOP LEFT):

dawn over Wingland Marsh

moonrise, Gedney Marsh

River Welland, Fosdyke Bridge

salt marsh and mudflats, Freiston Shore

RIGHT: **daffodils cut and packed for market, Whaplode Fen**

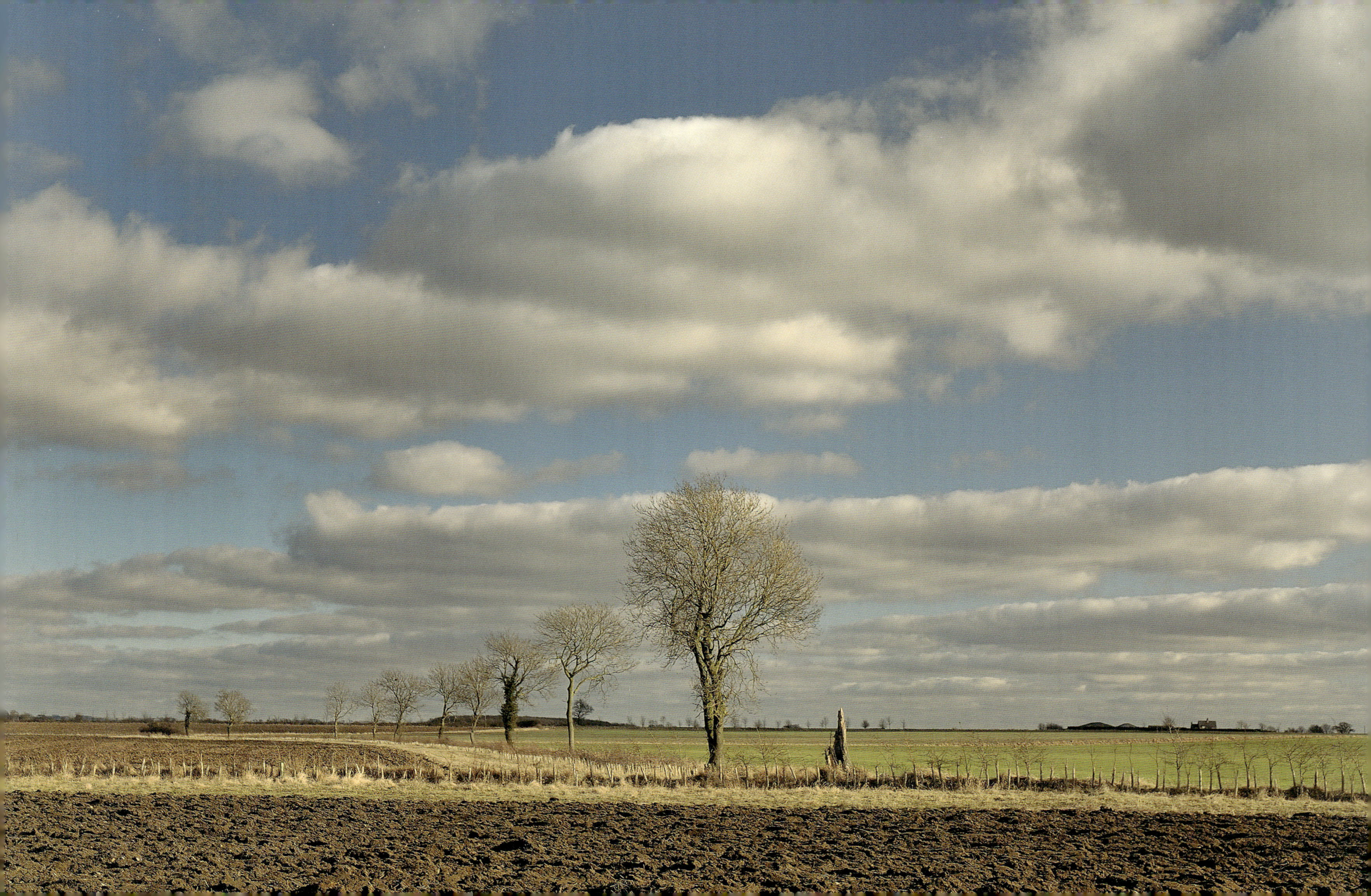

VI - MID LINDSEY VALE

Lying between the uplands of the Lincoln Cliff and the Wolds is an area of lowland that forms one of Lincolnshire's least explored landscapes. It is quiet and unobtrusive even by Lincolnshire standards – so much so that it has no name either locally or on Ordnance Survey maps and has thus been given rather prosaic titles by geographers and geologists such as Central Lincolnshire Vale or Lincolnshire Clay Vale. This book opts for Mid Lindsey Vale which, if not exactly poetic, is descriptive and concise.

The Mid Lindsey Vale runs for over 40 miles (64km) from the Humber in the north to Coningsby and East Kirkby in the south where it meets the Fens. Travelling southwards it gradually widens, from less than 2 miles (3.2km) at Ferriby Sluice to a maximum of some 12 miles (19.3km) between Lincoln and Horncastle. This occurs as the bounding edge of the Wolds trends south-east to create increasing separation from the Cliff. From Lincoln to Tattershall the Vale narrows again as the Witham Fens intrude from the south-west and divide it from the Lincoln Heath.

On first acquaintance namelessness seems almost appropriate for the Vale, which is Lincolnshire at its least demonstrative. Most of it is gently undulating clay farmland, never quite flat and never quite hilly, and almost wholly lacking in obvious features. This is a landscape of determined ordinariness where even the villages seem to shun attention and the only topographic drama is provided by the scarpline of the Wolds to the west. There are no soaring spires to match Lincolnshire's other lowlands, no impressive monuments except Tattershall Castle and no major country house to attract tourism. Likewise, the main towns of the Vale – Brigg, Market Rasen and Horncastle – are modestly attractive rather than flamboyant in their architecture. However, this does not mean that the Vale lacks identity or is unworthy of attention. Its landscape typically possesses a demure, slumbering charm and has considerable natural and historic interest, as well as being far more varied than is apparent from

FACING PAGE: **clay farmland near Cold Hanworth**

RIGHT: **Stainfield church**

a passing vehicle. Taken as a whole the area can even be described as the heart of Lincolnshire, given its central location, mix of landscape types and proximity to most of Lincolnshire's other defining landmarks and landscapes, including Lincoln, the Wolds, the River Witham and the Fens. Other notable assets include Lincolnshire's only offshore island – Read's Island in the Humber – and its own Victorian spa town at Woodhall Spa.

Geologically the Vale is underpinned by Jurassic clays but these are hidden across most of the area by later deposits from the Ice Age and after. By far the most widespread is glacial clay or till left by ice sheets and usually ascribed to a glacial period around 250 – 300 million years ago termed the Wolfstonian. This forms the surface across a great expanse of land stretching from Lincoln and Market Rasen through Wragby to Horncastle and beyond, and also survives in a more eroded form along the sides of the Ancholme valley between Market Rasen and Brigg.

Tills support the landscape most associated with the Vale, which is a gently undulating farmland of hedged fields and woods broken periodically by the shallow valleys of the main rivers and their tributary brooks (here called becks). Small villages and scattered brick farmsteads complete this basic picture. Today it is predominantly arable but retains occasional

TOP LEFT: **ash and willow, Dunholme Beck**

LEFT: **mud and stud cottage, Sotby**

FACING PAGE: **Vale countryside in summer, Scrivelsby**

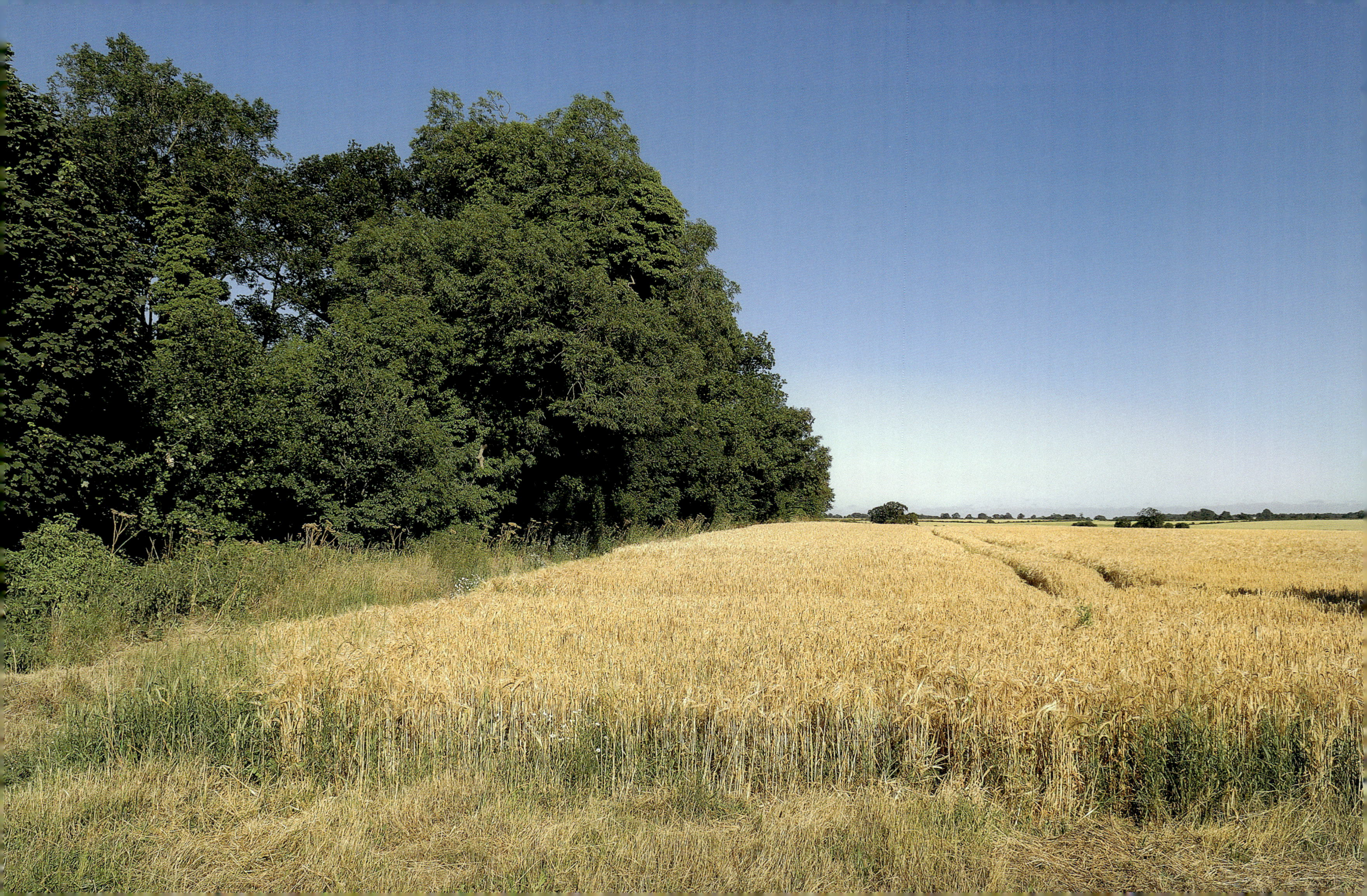

Bardney Limewoods is a National Nature Reserve (NNR) consisting of thirteen woodlands with SSSI status and is the most important survival of Small-leaved lime woodland in Britain. Since 2005 the NNR has been the core of a wider project area called the Lincolnshire Limewoods. This seeks to protect and link the woods as part of a landscape-scale approach to conserving the area's natural and historic value.

TOP LEFT: **woodland stream, Cocklode Wood**

ABOVE: **Greater butterfly orchid, Great West Wood**

LEFT: **Small-leaved lime, Chambers Farm Wood**

pastures and meadows as a reminder of its earlier farming history as an area of livestock and mixed husbandry. Other landscape features have also partially survived the post-1945 changes in farming including historic field patterns dating to enclosure – both early and Parliamentary – and their hedges and trees. Ash is by far the commonest hedgerow tree while willows are an attractive feature along the becks.

The south of the till country between Wragby and Stixwould is much more wooded and contains the woodland group called the Bardney Limewoods, with its population of Small-leaved lime and associated ecology. Here the fields are typically larger while the woodlands form blocks in the landscape that give a greater sense of enclosure than further north.

In complete contrast to the tills are areas of sand and gravel that support a landscape of heathland, pine plantations, golf courses and relatively poor farming. These deposits are of varying age and origin but most are associated with the Ice Age and its aftermath. Ice sheets are thought to have blocked both the Humber and the Wash at least once during the final or Devensian glaciation, causing meltwaters to pond back as large lakes. Known by geologists as Lake Humber and Lake Fenland these would have submerged virtually all of inland Lincolnshire except the uplands and were probably joined via the Lincoln Gap when at their maximum height. At the southern end of the Vale, adjoining the Witham Fens, sand and gravel deposits are closely linked to Lake Fenland and a complex fluvial history. This included periods of diversion of Trent waters as glacial fluctuation in

RIGHT: **Scots pine, Linwood Warren**

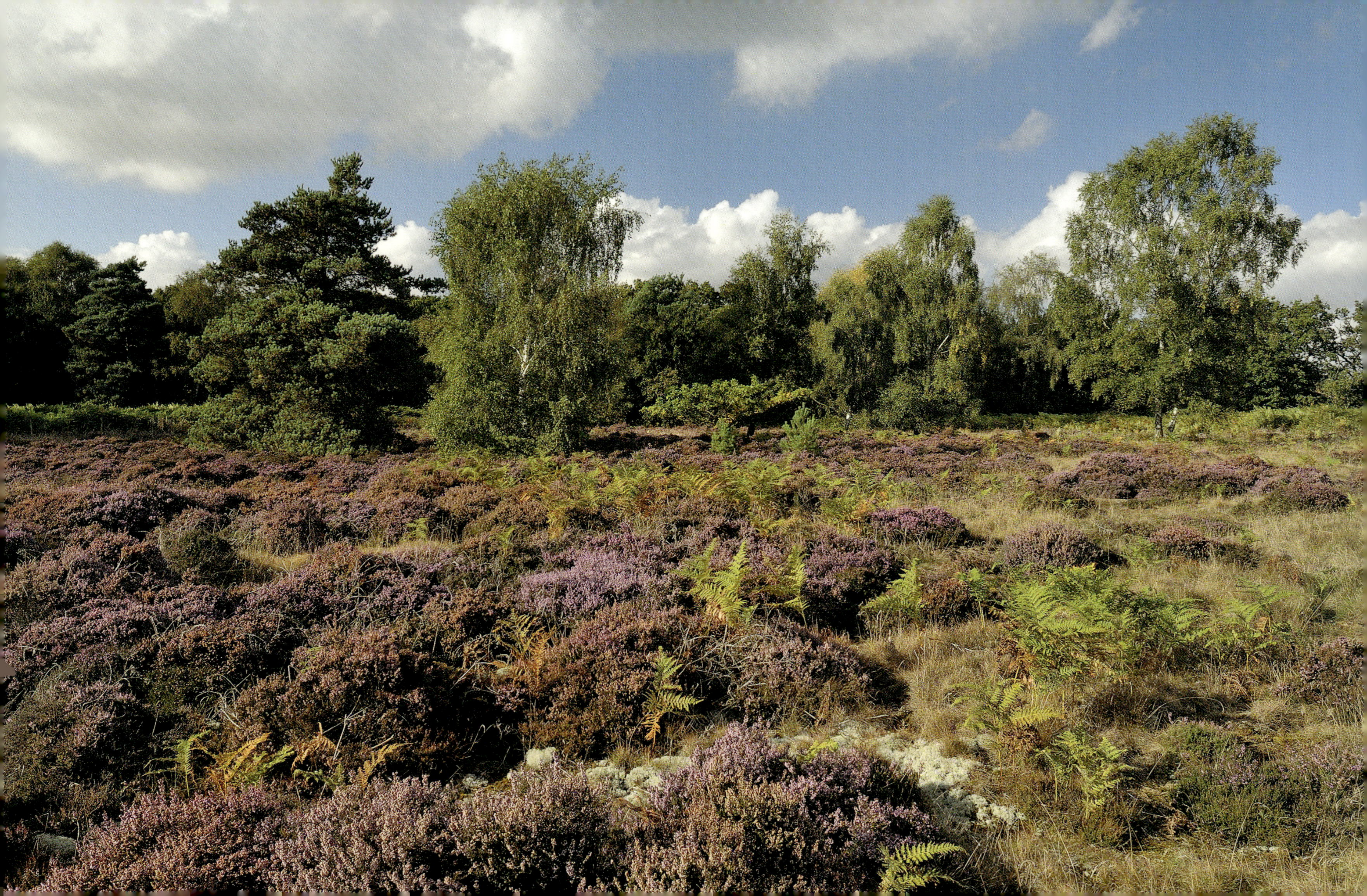

the Humber and Wash alternately blocked and allowed drainage to the North Sea. The large area of sand and gravel east of Woodhall Spa is thought to have been deposited by the River Bain as an outwash plain or delta in Lake Fenland and consists of material carried down from the Wolds. Today it supports a landscape of 'moors' and pine plantations, including the largest area of unreclaimed heathland in Lincolnshire at Kirkby Moor.

After the glaciers finally retreated and their lakes drained away, windblown Coversands were deposited extensively across the Vale and accumulated beneath the escarpment of the Wolds. Subsequent erosion has removed these deposits from many areas but they survive around Elsham and in a large tract stretching from Grasby to Market Rasen. As elsewhere in Lincolnshire, much of the Coversands heathland has been lost over the past two centuries and the surviving fragments are now protected and managed mainly for nature conservation.

The northern section of the Vale is occupied by the flatlands of the Ancholme valley. Here, Devensian glacial ice blocking the Humber Gap created another lake that gradually silted up leaving the lacustrine deposits

FACING PAGE & TOP RIGHT: **Kirkby Moor Nature Reserve.** Sands and gravels near Woodhall Spa support extensive heathlands of heather and acid grassland that are now protected for wildlife. Kirkby Moor's ecology is similar to that of the Coversands further north but its flora also includes southern species found in the Breckland of East Anglia. Notable fauna recorded on the reserve include woodlark, hobby, nightjar, adder and slow worm as well as 175 species of moth.

RIGHT: **Devil's-bit scabious (Succisa pratensis), Moor Farm**

ABOVE: **New River Ancholme and Brown's Bridge, Snitterby Carr**

FACING PAGE: **Ancholme Carrs near Cadney**

that form parts of the present valley floor. With rising sea levels after the final glaciation, the valley then evolved as a wetland area over millennia with deposition of both tidal and river silts and the localised development of peat in freshwater swamp conditions. Known as 'carrs' – the north Lincolnshire term equivalent to 'fens' – these wetlands occupied almost the entire floor of the Vale north of Brigg to the Humber and also continued southwards along the Ancholme valley as far as Bishopbridge.

Drainage of the Ancholme Carrs was undertaken in the 1630s and 40s in response to flooding from the Humber and involved the construction of a new straight channel from Bishopbridge to the Humber and a new sluice at South Ferriby. As elsewhere, there was conflict between the drainers – in this case a group of gentry Adventurers led by Sir John Monson and supported by the Crown – and village communities such as Winterton which stood to lose common grazing rights on the drained carrs. Sabotage of the Ferriby Sluice in the Civil War left the carrs drowned again for a century until its restoration and further drainage works were undertaken.

The Ancholme's former winding course survives in places as a small stream and in the valley's parish boundaries, while the drained wetlands still retain their carr place names linked to the adjoining villages. Today the carrs are predominantly in arable use.

Early human occupation of the Vale is thought to have focused initially on the lighter soils of the Coversands and other sands and gravels, especially

159

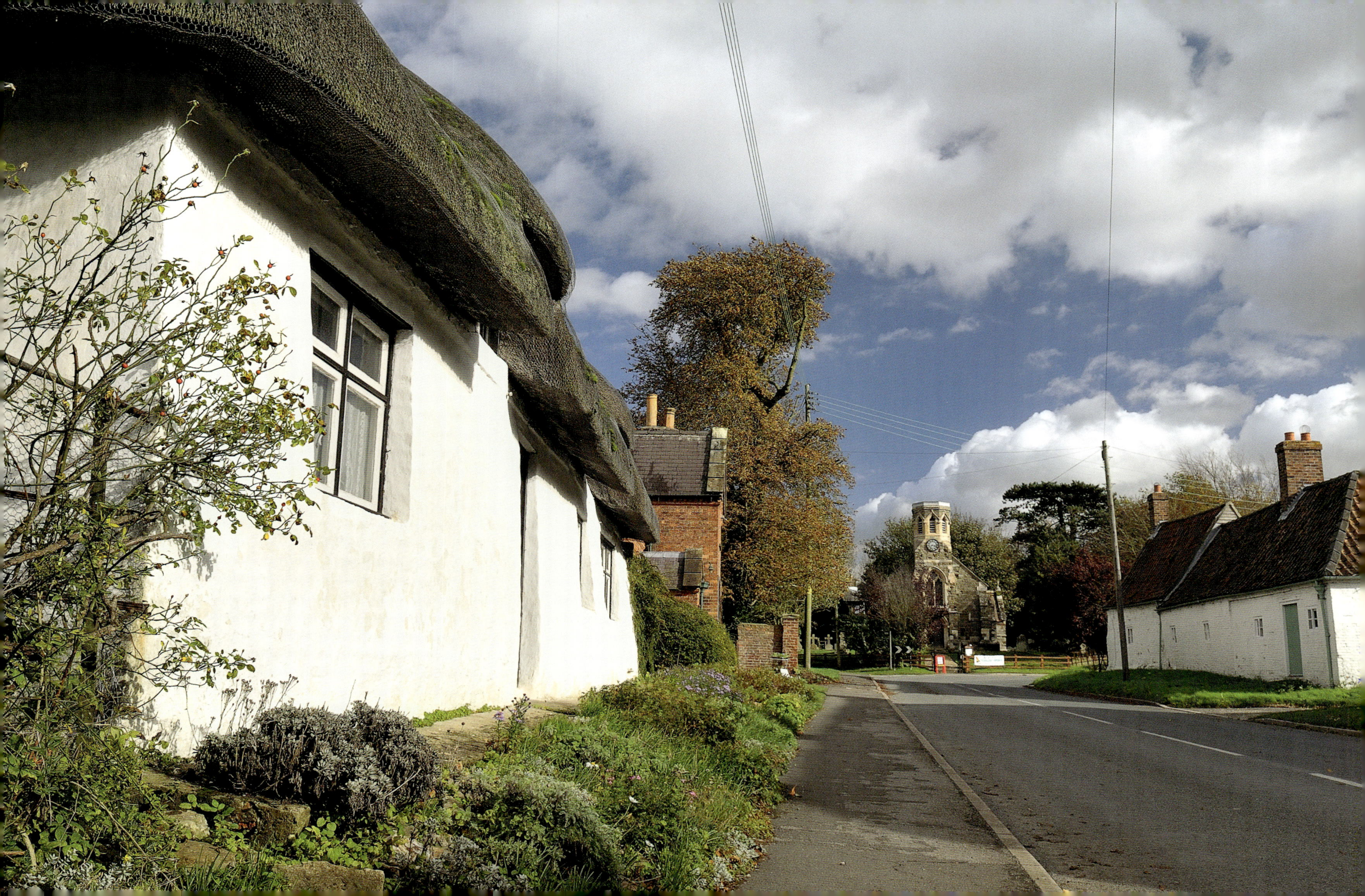

along the fen/carr edges of the Witham and Ancholme valleys. The latter provided suitable locations for settlement and early farming with access to a range of resources. Occupation of the heavier clay soils occurred later with the expansion of agriculture and ploughing.

The present-day settlement pattern of the Vale corresponds essentially to the Domesday Survey of 1086 though numerous shrunken and deserted Medieval villages exist, especially on the clays. The creation of Woodhall Spa as a resort from the 1830s is an isolated case of a post-Medieval addition. Medieval village settlement forms loose lines along the Ancholme valley edges while a looser, more scattered pattern exists on the clays south of Market Rasen.

The Vale's traditional domestic and farm buildings are predominantly of brick and pantile, though a good scattering of mud and stud construction also survives in the villages, as at Thimbleby. Churches are typically modest by Lincolnshire standards and display a variety of building materials sourced from either the Wolds or Cliff, with brick in the remoter clay areas.

The Fen edge along the Witham valley has a concentration of monastic sites including Barlings, Bardney, Tupholme, Stixwould and Kirkstead, some of which retain ruined buildings. Most of these sites show continuity with pre-Christian sacred use including prehistoric ritual causeways into the fens.

FACING PAGE: **Thimbleby village**

RIGHT: **Barlings Abbey**

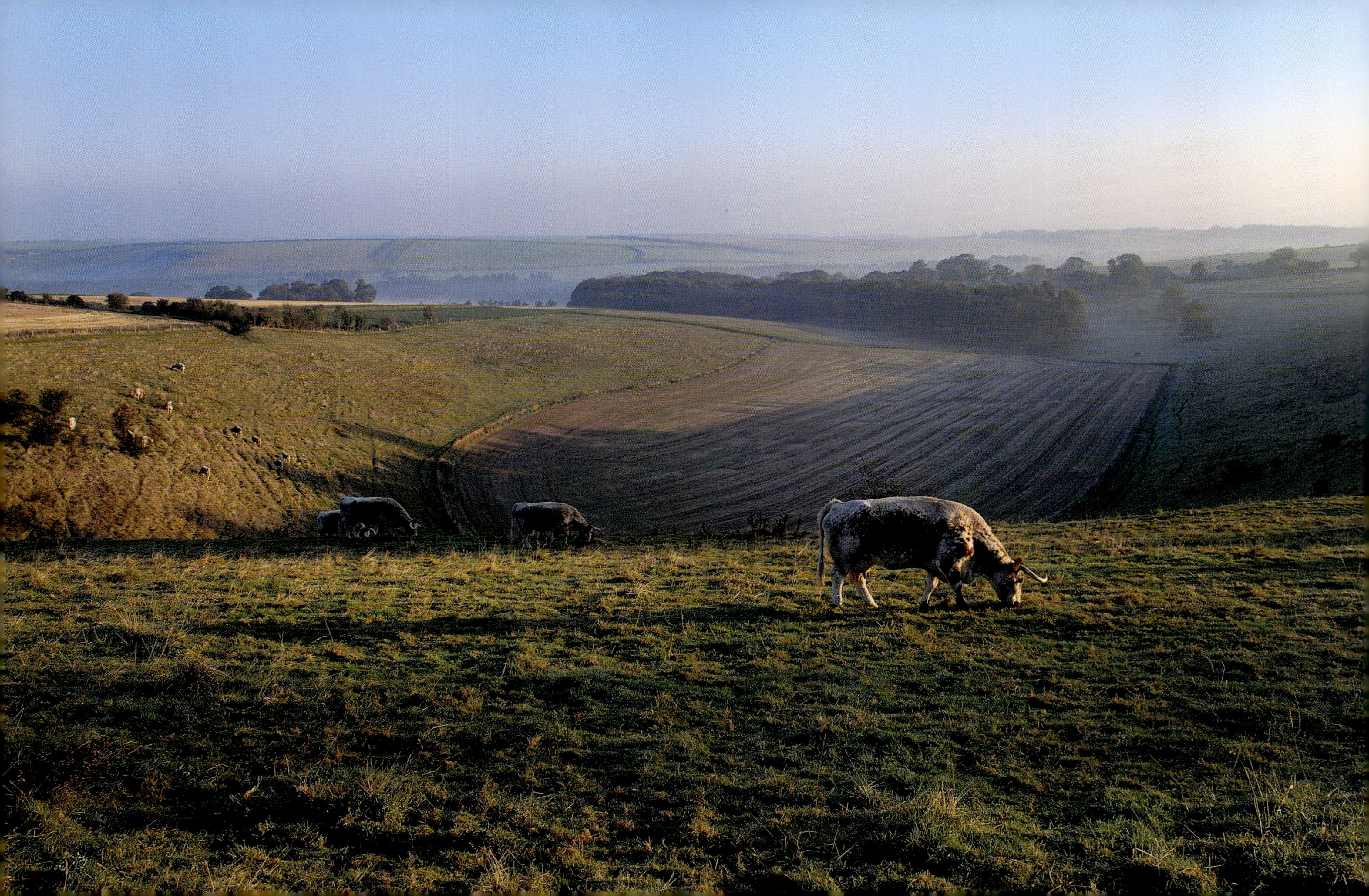

VII - WOLDS

Chalk landscapes in England are closely associated with the downs and coast of southern counties such as Sussex and Dorset but a belt of chalk country also extends northwards from the Chilterns through East Anglia and on into Lincolnshire and east Yorkshire. This northern chalk limb has been breached over geological time by the Wash and the Humber and is consequently articulated into distinct sections that form the East Anglian chalklands, the Lincolnshire Wolds and the Yorkshire Wolds. This chapter covers the chalk and its associated rocks within Lincolnshire, where the Wolds form the county's hilliest landscape.

The Wolds are generally considered to be the scenic highlight of the Lincolnshire countryside and, despite the appeal made in this book for greater appreciation of Lincolnshire's flatlands, it would be perverse not to recognise their specialness. Nowhere else in Lincolnshire has the sense of being a true upland with a bold topography of ridges, hills and valleys. The Wolds are not spectacular by the standards of Cumbria, the Pennines or the West Country, but there is drama and grandness in their swelling contours and sweeping vistas. They include the highest land in eastern England between Kent and Yorkshire, reaching 550 ft (168m) at Normanby Top, and offer Lincolnshire's most extensive views. On a clear day most of Lincolnshire's other landscape character areas can be seen and the far horizons extend beyond to Norfolk, Holderness, the Yorkshire Wolds and the Pennines. To complete the upland picture, the Wolds have noticeably harder winters than the surrounding lowlands, including more days of snowfall and lying snow.

Like most of Lincolnshire's landscape character areas, the Wolds are strongly linear in their overall morphology. They form a belt of upland running for over 40 miles (64km) from the Humber to the Fens, yet are only 8 miles (13km) wide at most. In basic terms they resemble the

FACING PAGE: **chalk contours near Worlaby at dawn**

RIGHT: **ploughed chalk field near Hallington**

Jurassic limestone upland to the west in being a 'cuesta' landform created by tectonic uplift and tilting of sedimentary rocks. This has given rise to a steep western scarp overlooking the Mid Lindsey Vale and an upland plateau that inclines much more gradually eastwards towards the Lincolnshire Marsh. However, the Wolds are more deeply incised by streams than most of the Jurassic limestone belt and consequently have a hillier topography. Conversely, the only complete breach of the Wolds between the Humber and The Wash is the relatively minor Kirmington Gap, which is used by the road and rail routes to Grimsby and Cleethorpes and which separates off the northernmost part of the Wolds.

Within this broad picture the Wolds display considerable variation in geology and character. Chalk is just one of a series of Cretaceous rocks that make up the area, though it is by far the most widely exposed. It forms the surface throughout the northern and central Wolds and also runs continuously along their eastern side. In the southern Wolds and along the western escarpment, however, the chalk has been stripped away by erosion to reveal underlying sandstones, ironstones and clays. As explained below, this variety is manifested in contrasting landscapes.

The characteristic landscape of the chalk is a smooth plateau incised by east-flowing valleys that are dry in their upper part. The classic landforms associated with chalk can all be seen here to some degree including

LEFT: **roadside beech trees near Thoresway**

FACING PAGE: **snowy track, Risby Top**

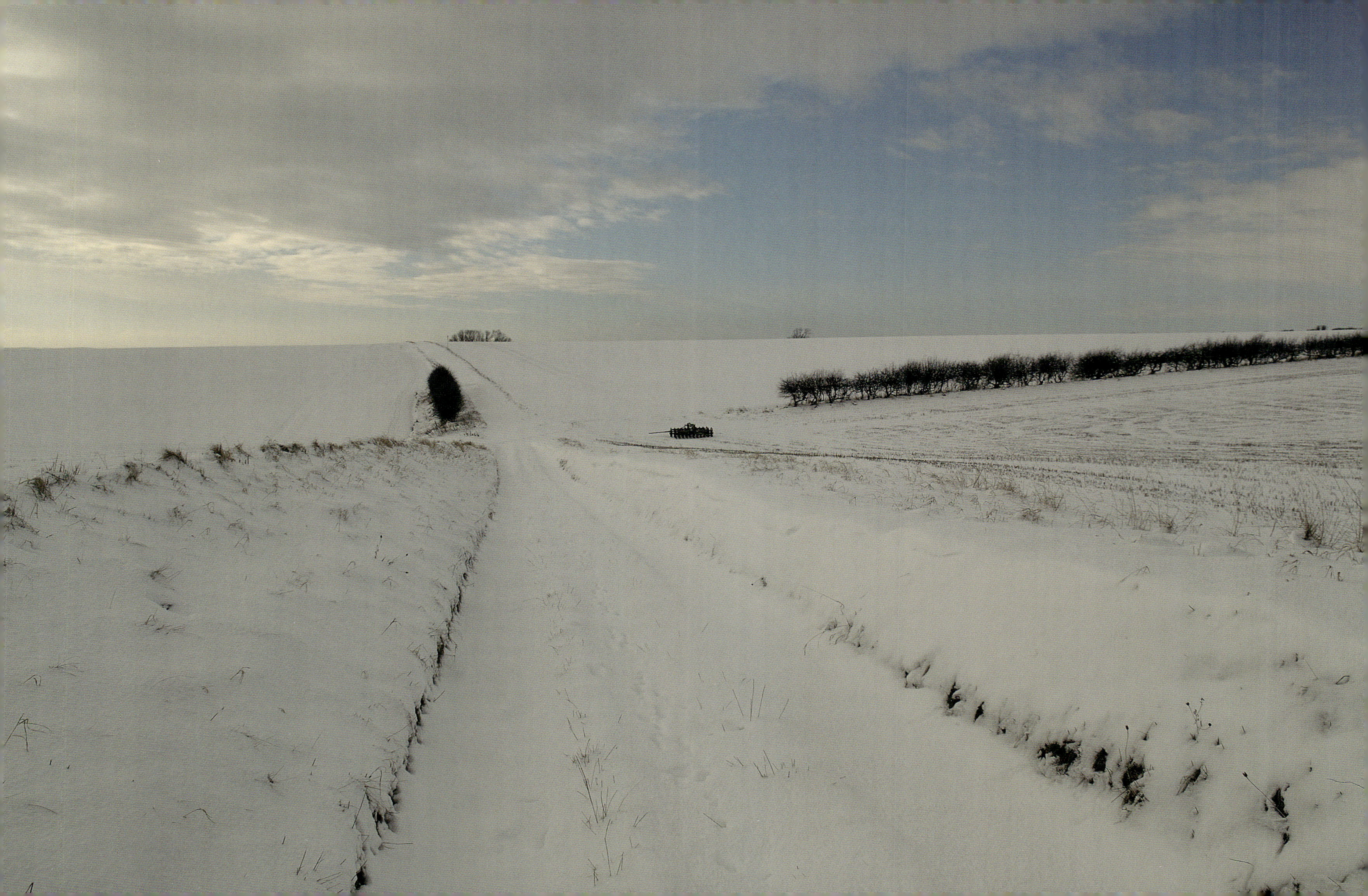

Arable farming gives a distinctive surface to the chalk Wolds that is particularly striking when the stony soils are exposed by ploughing. Fragments of chalk lend the soil its colour which is usually off-white, though a basal band of red chalk can be seen in fields along the western scarp of the Wolds. Most of the chalk plateau has been cultivated since the Agricultural Revolution of the late 18th and early 19th centuries and chalk grassland is now restricted to a few locations on valley sides, along the scarp and in former quarries.

ABOVE: **undulating chalk landscape near Withcall**

LEFT: **chalk contours near Swallow**

convex slopes, wave-like undulations and steep-sided combes. However, the Lincolnshire Wolds differ from the chalk downs of southern England in having been moulded directly by ice sheets during the last Ice Age. This has added a distinctive northern accent to their geomorphology including ice-smoothed surfaces, glacial meltwater channels and areas where the surface is covered by till or other glacial deposits. Along the eastern edge of the Wolds, the chalk forms a relict coastal cliff overlooking the Marsh. This has been smoothed by glacial action and buried under till in the final or Devensian glaciation, but still drops sharply to the coastal flatlands.

A second distinctive feature of the Lincolnshire chalk is that all but the steepest slopes have been ploughed for over two centuries. Before the Agricultural Revolution much of the high chalk plateau was unreclaimed grassland similar to that on the Lincoln Heath and also used mainly for rough grazing and rabbit warrening. By 1850, reclamation and enclosure of the grasslands, coupled with the new 'corn and sheep' rotation, had transformed the chalk Wolds into highly productive farmland of national repute for its High Farming regime. Today the chalk Wolds are still predominantly under the plough, though 'corn and sheep' farming has been replaced since 1945 by purely arable production focusing on cereals, rapeseed and sugar beet. Nevertheless, much of the landscape of the enclosure period has survived agricultural change, including large fields with hawthorn hedges, small blocks of woodland and isolated farmsteads. The valleys tend to have more woodland and a less exposed feel as well as containing most of the villages. Except in the dry valley heads the streams

RIGHT: **a chalk spring in the central Wolds**

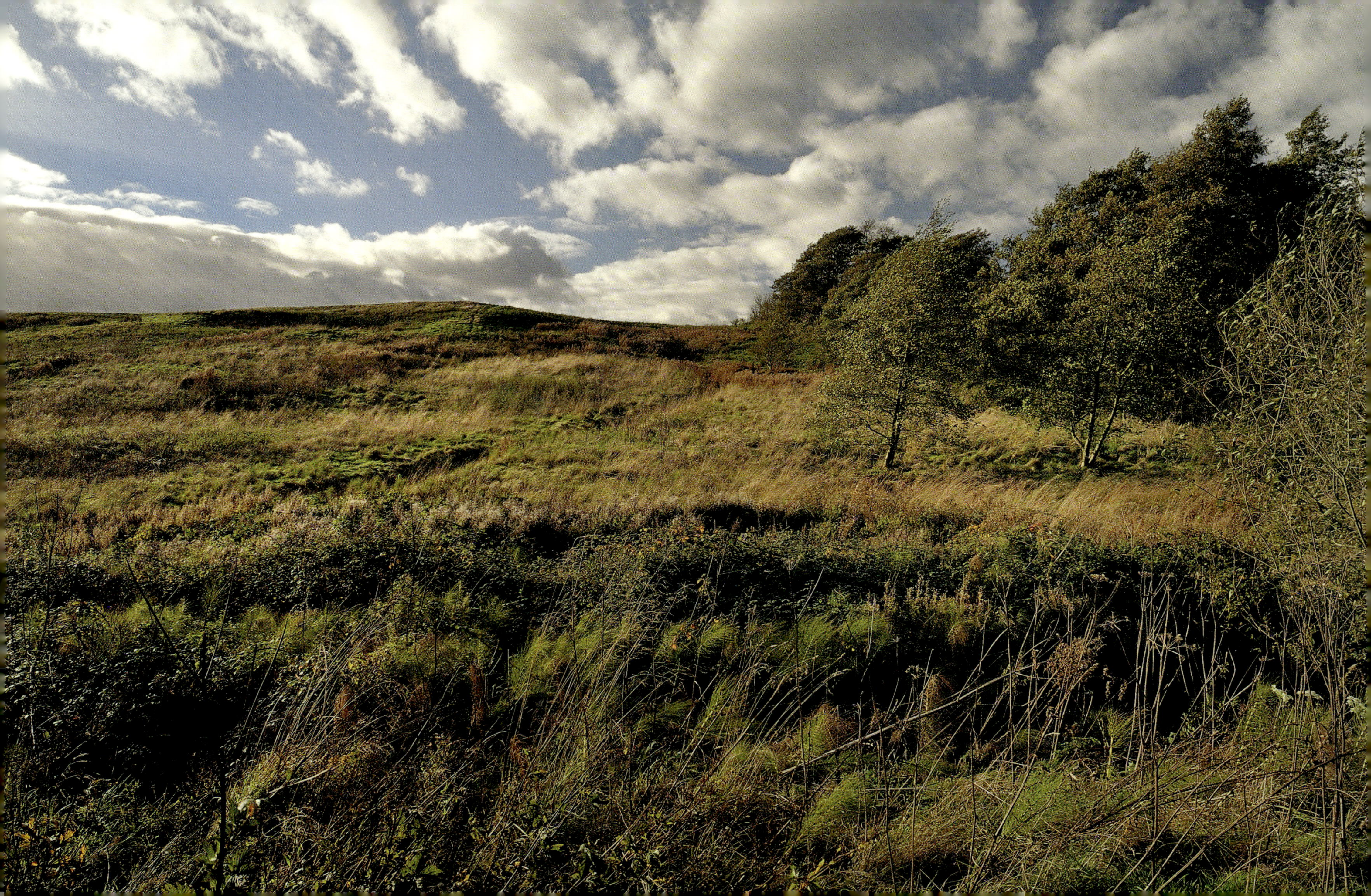

have typically cut through the chalk into the less porous rocks beneath, giving rise to a distinct valley bottom landscape of meadows, ornamental lakes and wet areas of undrained carr that are often wooded.

The southern Wolds have a completely different character from the chalk country further north. Here the Lower Cretaceous rocks lie at the surface, mainly ironstones and sandstones, including the distinctive green-hued Spilsby Sandstone. Between Horncastle and Spilsby these rocks create an attractive, broken hillcountry centred on the Lymn valley. The hills surrounding the valley are capped by the harder sandstones and ironstones but have been fretted by numerous streams and glacial meltwater to expose softer rocks in steep-sided valleys, such as Snipe Dales and Sow Dale. The River Lymn itself has cut down as far as the underlying Jurassic clays. This area is one of Lincolnshire's most intimate landscapes – secretive, damp and bosky – with small fields, quiet villages and sandstone churches set amongst trees. In contrast to the arid paleness of the chalk Wolds, soils here are rich browns and reds and there is more grassland and rough pasture.

The boundaries of the Wolds are also varied and distinctive. The western scarp is the highest in Lincolnshire and certainly its most imposing landscape feature. The section between Nettleton and Claxby is particularly dramatic,

FACING PAGE: **Sow Dale**

ABOVE RIGHT: **mud and stud at Bag Enderby**

RIGHT: **Spilsby Sandstone masonry, Tetford church**

with rough grassland and quarried land giving an almost Pennine quality. Geologically the scarp varies considerably throughout its length. North of Caistor it is a single slope composed mainly of chalk, while southwards the Lower Cretaceous strata outcrop below a chalk cap to give a compound scarp that is complicated further by landslips and valleys cutting into it, including Nettleton Beck. As the Lower Cretaceous outcrop increases south of Ludford, the scarp splits into two. The chalk retains a distinct edge that pushes south-east from Donington-on-Bain to Candlesby and is often wooded or down-like. The Lower Cretaceous scarp is less defined, being broken by the Bain valley and often covered by till. However, along the southern edge of the Wolds, around Old Bolingbroke and the Keals, the Spilsby Sandstone forms bolder hills rising from the Fens. These are thought to be the eroded remains of former sea cliffs that existed during an interglacial period around 100,000 years ago when sea levels were much higher than at present. Here, West Keal church is particularly noteworthy for its hilltop setting and wide panorama across the Fens including Boston and the Wash.

At the other extremity of the Wolds, the upland ridge drops suddenly to the River Humber in a landscape scarred by chalk quarries and old clay pits, and

ABOVE: **Walesby church on the western scarp of the Wolds**

FACING PAGE: **Nettleton Beck**

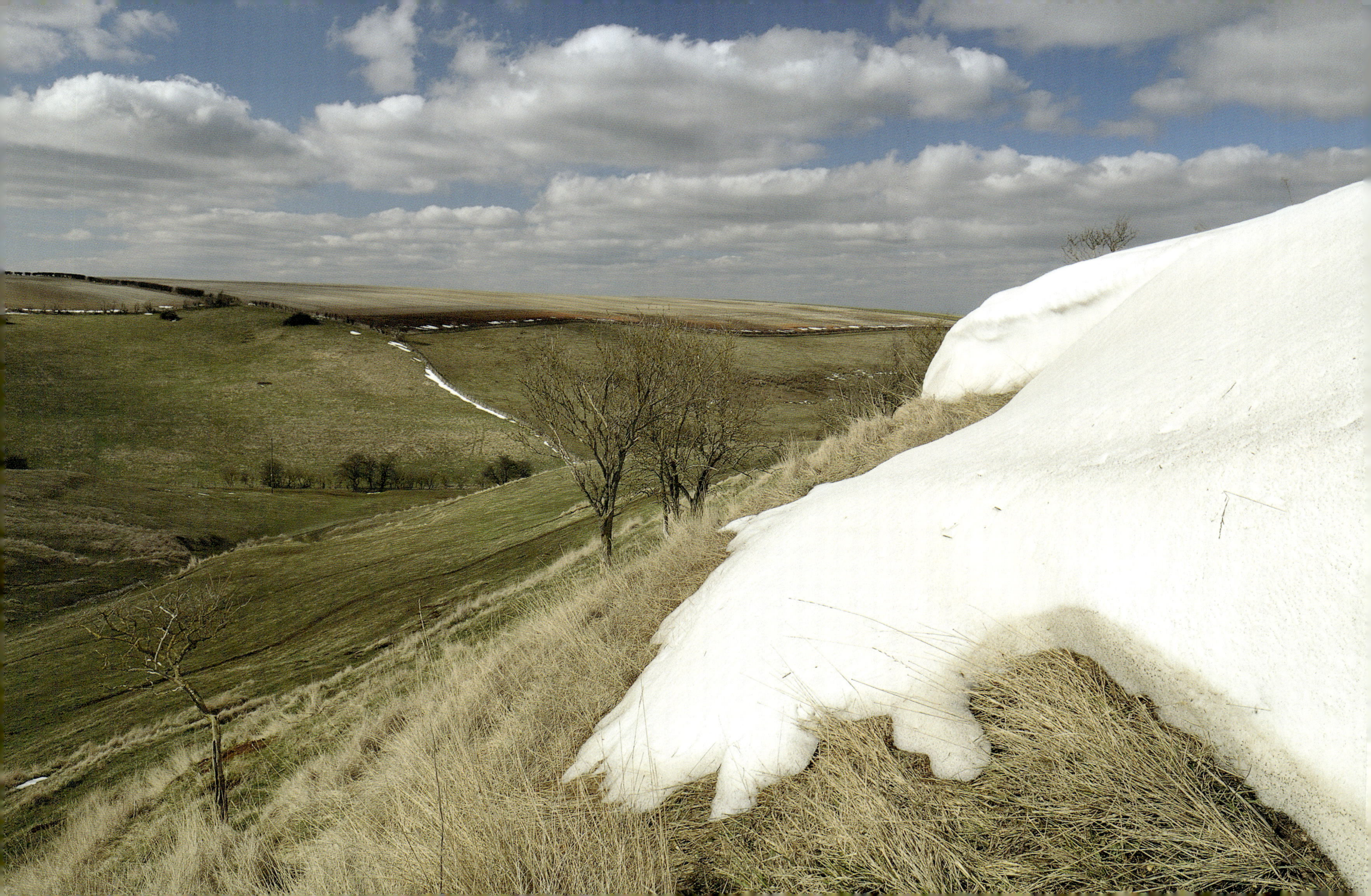

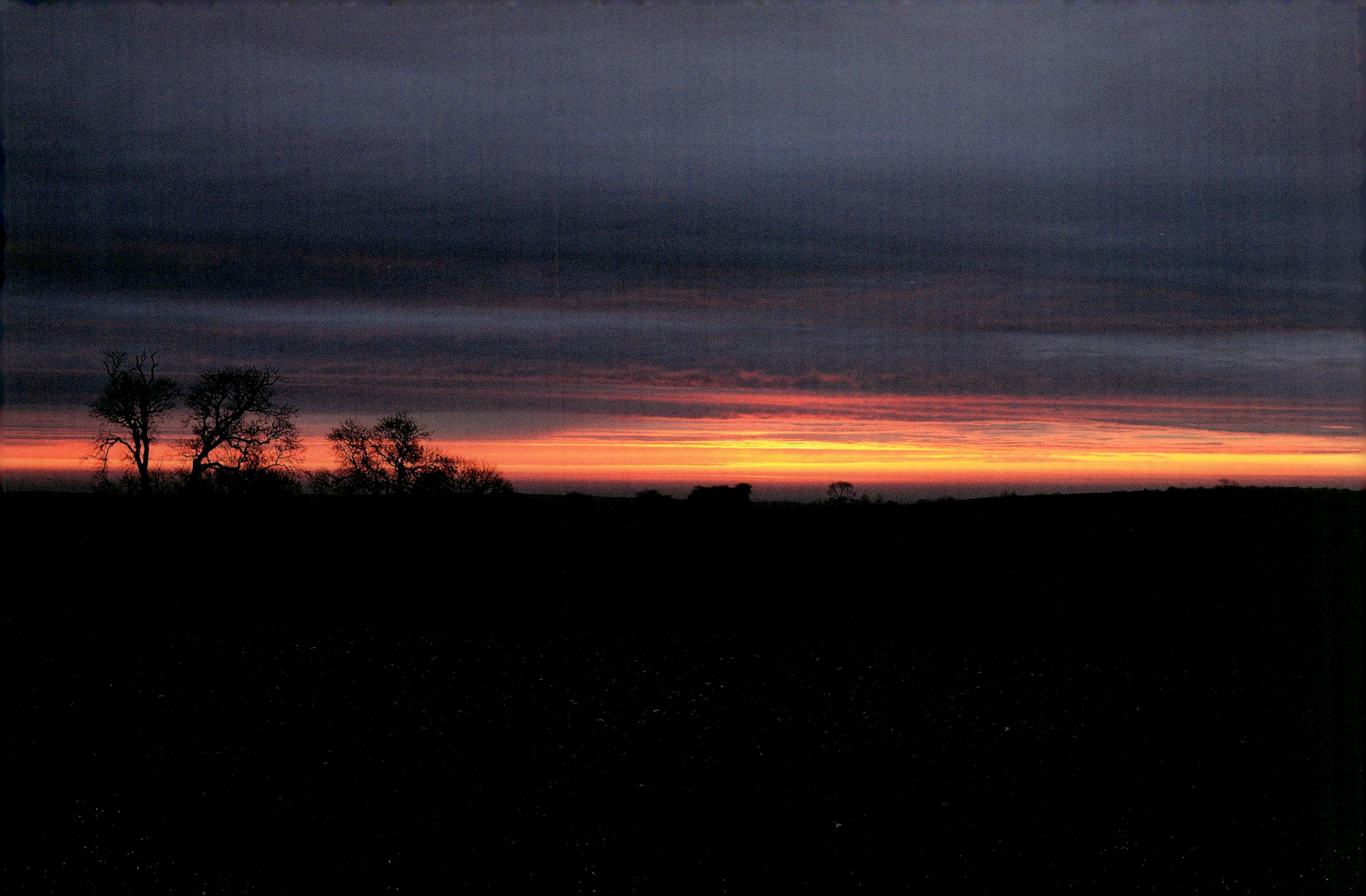

offers views across to Yorkshire and the chalk hills of the Yorkshire Wolds, which form the opposite side of the Humber Gap.

The Wolds are the richest area in Lincolnshire for prehistoric archaeology and include finds from all periods. Early stone tools from the Palaeolithic have been found beneath glacial deposits at Welton-le-Wold and in the Kirmington Gap and probably relate to seasonal hunting activity in steppe or tundra conditions. As conditions ameliorated following the final glacial retreat, Mesolithic hunter-gathering focused on transition zones, leaving concentrations of flint tools in the southern Wolds and their Fen edge.

Farming and forest clearance on the Wolds probably began around 6,000 years ago and included both cultivation and animal husbandry. The Wolds have by far the greatest concentration of Neolithic long barrows in Lincolnshire with some 56 sites identified, probably reflecting the strong ritual significance of the uplands. Bronze Age round barrows are even more numerous with over 350 sites identified. Settlement and agriculture in the Wolds evolved gradually through the Iron Age and Romano-British periods, with the addition of villas quite late in the Roman occupation.

FACING PAGE: **dawn over the coast from near Maidenwell**

TOP RIGHT: **Bronze Age round barrow near Kirmond-le-Mire**

RIGHT: **rainclouds over chalk plateau, Haugham**

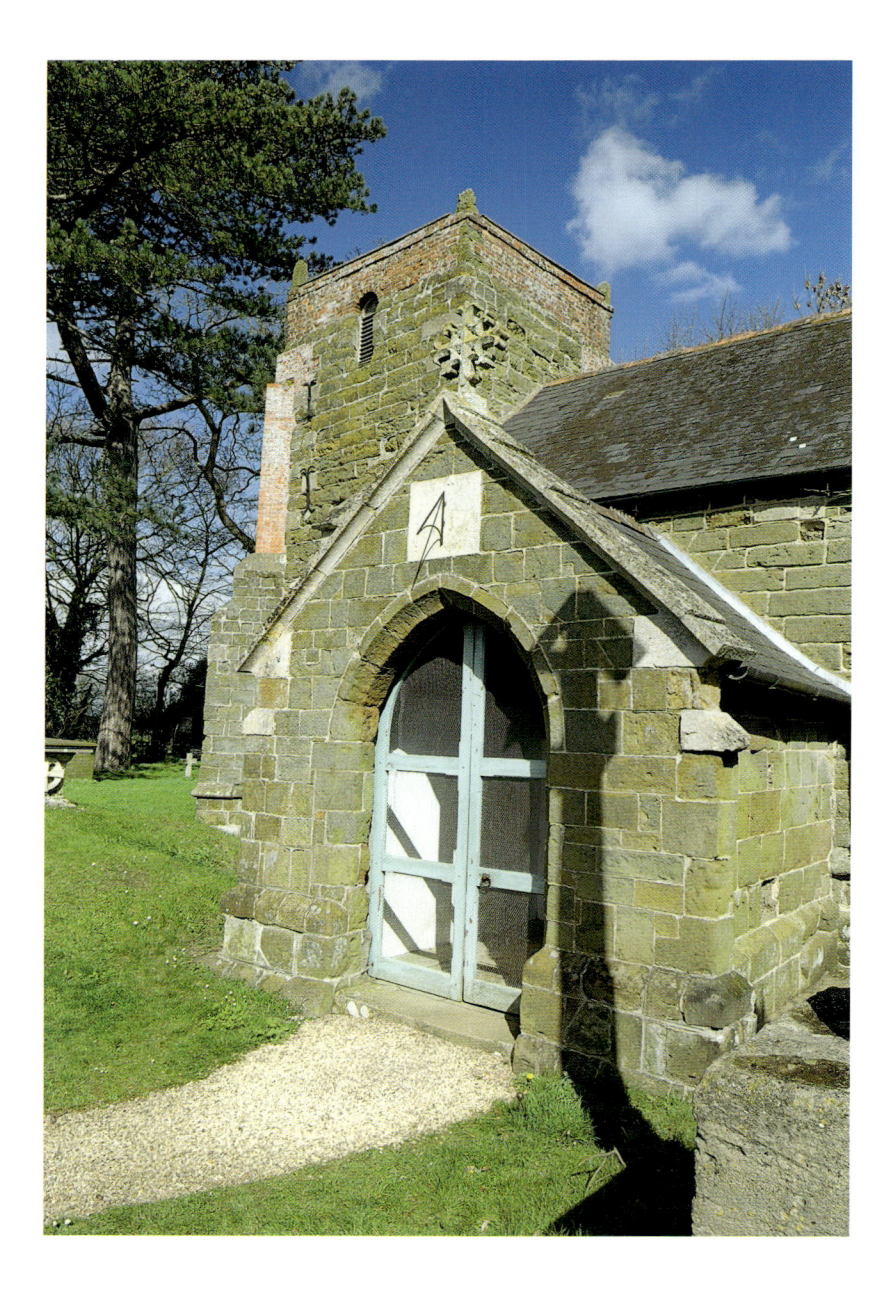

The Medieval settlement pattern in the Wolds is strongly nucleated, with the southern Wolds being more prosperous and heavily populated than the less fertile chalk areas to the north. Almost all present-day villages were already established by the Domesday Survey. However, there are over 70 deserted Medieval villages in the Wolds including several well-preserved sites such as North Ormsby and Calceby. Enclosure of the Wolds is split between early and Parliamentary phases with the latter accounting for the reclamation of the chalk plateau for intensive farming as noted above.

Traditional farm and domestic buildings in the Wolds are mainly of brick though local stone has sometimes been used where easily available and several villages have surviving mud and stud cottages. Most churches in the Wolds are modest by Lincolnshire standards, reflecting the area's relative lack of wealth in Medieval times. Country houses and their parks are also surprisingly modest though the vast landscaped Brocklesby estate in the northern Wolds is an emphatic exception.

Except in the extreme north, the Wolds are largely free from major 20th century development though the wartime radar station at Stenigot and modern telecommunications masts provide notable landmarks.

LEFT: **Somersby church.** Like many churches in the southern Wolds, St. Margaret's is built mainly in greenish-coloured Spilsby Sandstone. Other building stones used in the Wolds include a rich orange-brown ironstone and, occasionally, chalk. Somersby is famous as the home of the Tennyson family, where Alfred spent his youth and produced his early poetry.

ABOVE: **sunrise from the Bluestone Heath Road near Worlaby**

RIGHT: **mud and stud ruin in the Tennyson country**

VIII - MARSH & COAST

The area of lowland set between the Wolds and the North Sea is known as the Lincolnshire Marsh or Marshland. Very little of it is unreclaimed wetland today and most of the inland portion or Middle Marsh was historically never marshland. However, the name conveys well the broad sense of the area being adjacent to the sea and having a close relationship with the latter in its natural and human landscapes.

The Marshland is one of the largest of the landscape character areas in Lincolnshire, stretching north to south for nearly 50 miles (78km) from the Humber Bank to the Steeping River, and spanning 5 to 10 miles (8 to 10 km) in width throughout. Parts of it are dominated by urban growth, especially the area around Grimsby, which includes the holiday resort of Cleethorpes and the vast port and petrochemical developments at Immingham and Killingholme. Further south the discontinuous line of coastal resorts forms another focus of population from Mablethorpe to Skegness. Elsewhere the Marshland is still essentially rural and the market towns of Louth and Alford retain much of their traditional character and a distinctive feeling of being 'over the hills and far away'.

The character of the Marshland is often elusive and, despite being one of the most traversed parts of Lincolnshire, is probably amongst the least noticed as a landscape. Commercial and holiday traffic streams across the Marsh on its way to Grimsby and the coast, but few travellers see beyond the flatness to understand the area's distinctive history and character.

The Marshland divides geologically and historically into three distinct but linked landscapes; namely Middle Marsh, Outmarsh and Coast. These are described separately below, but the area's evolution as a coastal zone is worth outlining first. As noted previously, the Marshland is underpinned by a wave-cut chalk platform created by the erosion of a cliffed coastline along the eastern edge of the Wolds. Up to 300 ft (91m) high and similar

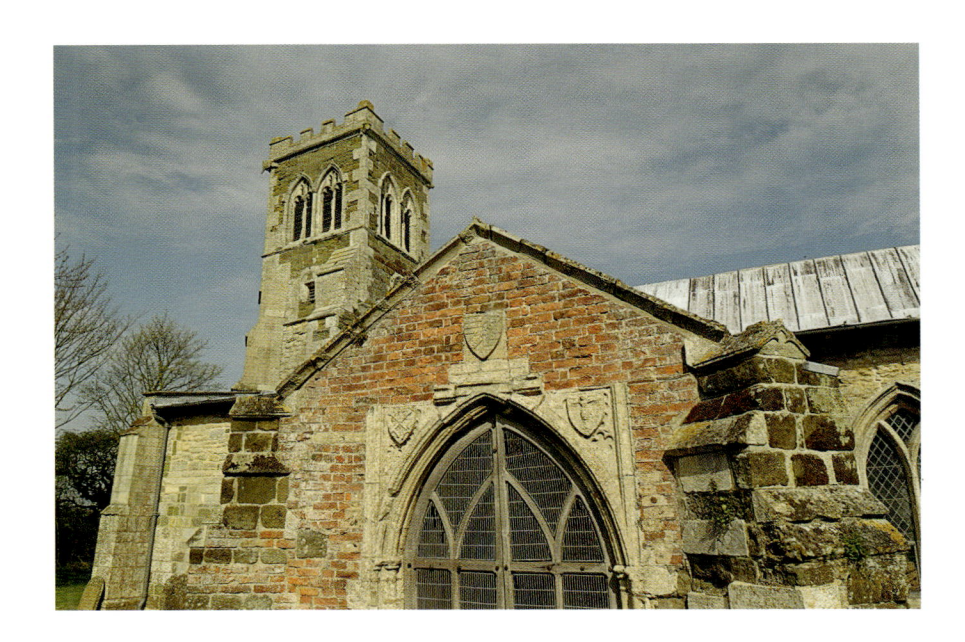

FACING PAGE: **sandy coast at Theddlethorpe St. Helen**

RIGHT: **Saltfleetby All Saints church**

in character to the present-day chalk cliffs of the Kent and Sussex coasts, this cliff last existed in the warm, interglacial conditions before the final or Devensian glaciation which buried it under till deposits. The tills lie directly on the chalk platform as far east as the modern coastline and beyond, extending under the sea into what was Doggerland. Outwash deposits from the glaciers also survive off the present coast as sandbanks which have historically contributed material to create Lincolnshire's sandy beaches and dune systems.

The Devensian tills provided the post-glacial surface that Mesolithic hunter-gatherers and trees recolonised as conditions warmed and the ice sheets retreated around 10,000 years ago. However, the subsequent rise in sea level gradually submerged Doggerland and pushed the coastline back inland, inundating the early forests and creating a wetland zone in the seaward part of the Marshland. The stumps of these trees can still be seen at low spring tides in places along the coast. Peat formation was followed by marshy silt deposits and finally from the late Roman period by a covering of tidal silt. As river gradients reduced, the early valleys that had cut into the tills also became silted and developed as floodplain wetlands. Human activity has subsequently modified this landscape with coastal defences

TOP LEFT: **North Sea at Anderby Creek**

LEFT: **artesian spring or 'blow well', Tetney**

FACING PAGE: **storm over the Marshland from near North Ormsby**

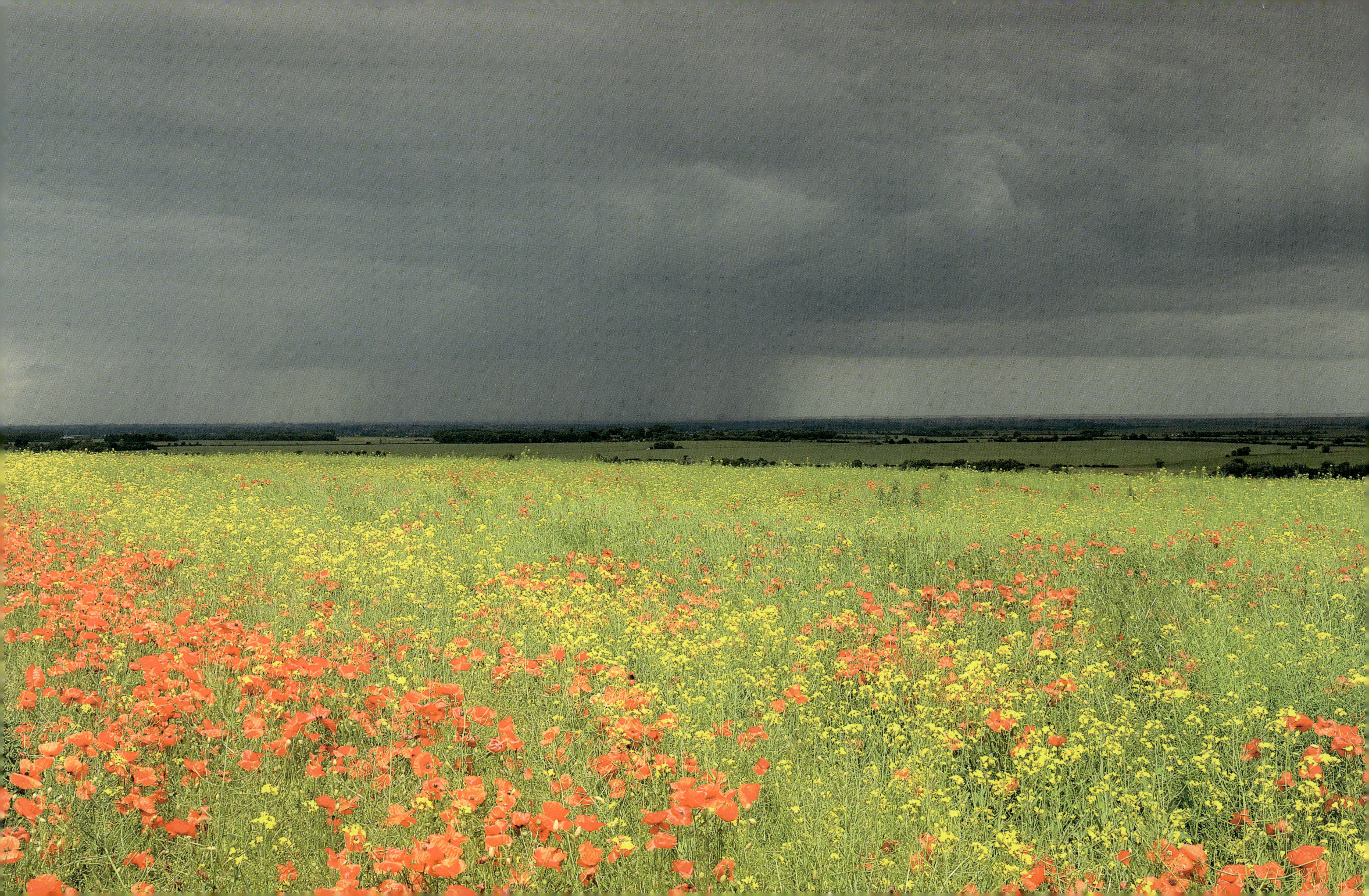

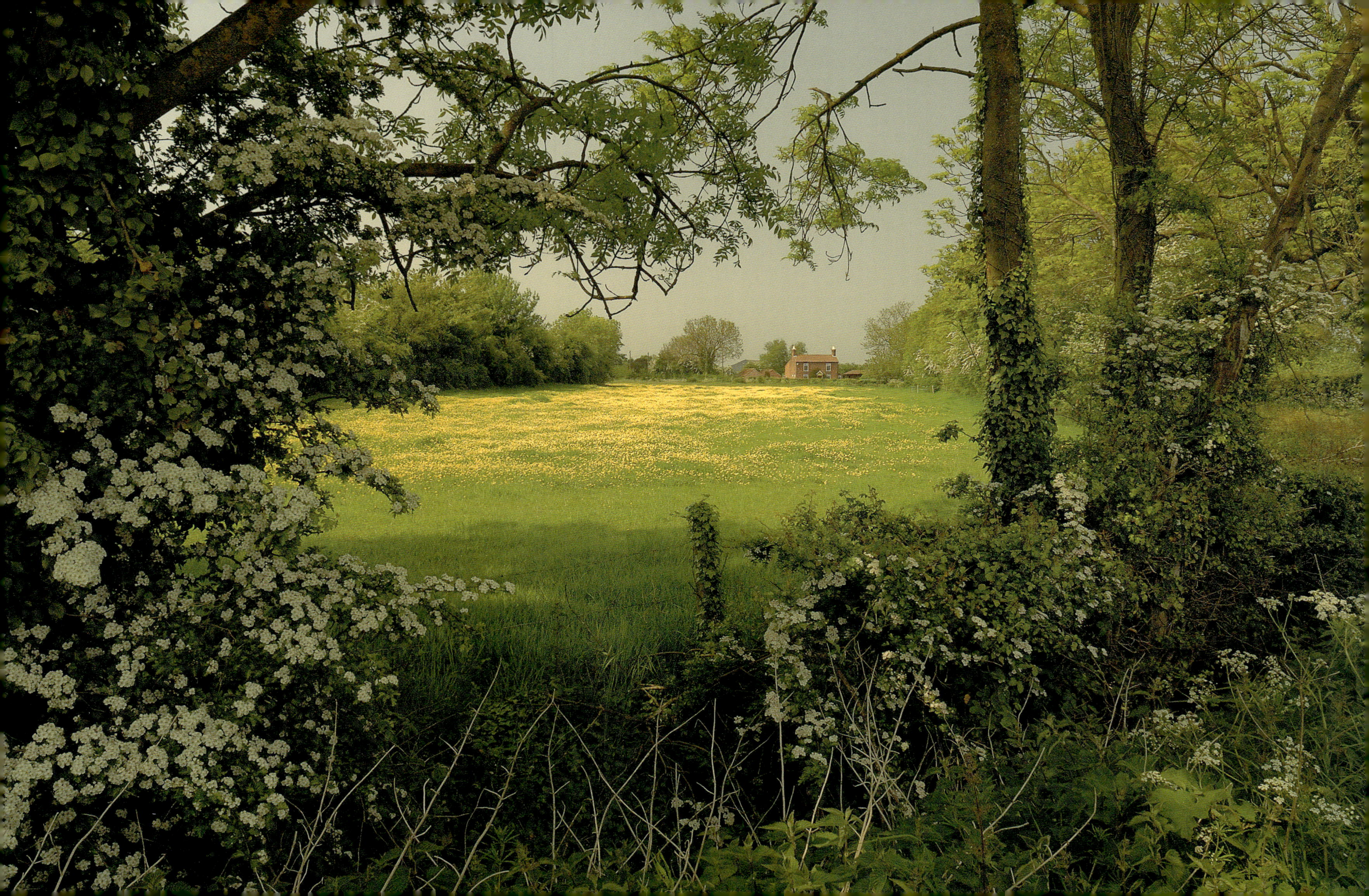

Before World War II, the Lincolnshire Marsh was characterised by mixed farming and permanent grassland covered more than 70% of the land in some Outmarsh parishes. Since then the area has experienced widespread field drainage and conversion of pasture and meadow to arable, with 25% of Outmarsh grassland having been ploughed between 1990 and 2000 alone. In 2003 the Lincolnshire Coastal Grazing Marshes Project was set up to conserve the pastoral landscapes and heritage of the Marshland and consolidate the best surviving areas of grazing marsh in partnership with local farmers and landowners. Traditionally-managed damp pasture and field ditches are an important wildlife habitat and the historic field patterns, ridge and furrow and other earthworks are integral to the landscape character of the Marshland.

FACING PAGE & BOTTOM RIGHT: **pastures near Orby**

RIGHT: **Outmarsh pasture with ridge and furrow, Saltfleetby All Saints.** The ridges here are wider than those found in Lincolnshire's uplands and vales but are clearly created by ploughing. They are therefore different in origin from the 'dylands' found in the Fens (see page 44).

and wetland drainage but the the overall pattern of the Marshland is still rooted firmly in its history of glaciation and coastal evolution.

The Middle Marsh forms a band of slightly undulating countryside adjoining the Wolds where the Devensian till still lies at the surface. Less pastoral than the Outmarsh it was nevertheless an area of mixed farming with some 40% of its farmland under grass in 1939. Today the landscape is dominated by arable farming within a framework of fields, winding lanes and woodland blocks that retains some but not all of its historic detail. Ash is the main tree of the hedgerows and woods in this area.

For most of its length Middle Marsh is sufficiently wide to support two distinct lines of settlement; one along the foot of the Wolds that includes Barrow-upon-Humber, Louth and Alford and the second, further east, marking the edge of dry land in early Medieval times. South of Alford, however, the pattern becomes fuzzier as the main band of till narrows towards Burgh-le-Marsh and scattered 'islands' of till of varying size push east towards the coast. These protrude slightly above the surrounding wetlands and therefore provided dry land for Anglo-Saxon and Danish settlement as at Hannah, Huttoft, Mumby and Hogsthorpe.

Except where the till surface reaches right to the sea at Grimsby and Cleethorpes, a low-lying zone of former wetland separates the Middle Marsh from the present coastline. This has a surface of mainly tidal silts deposited in salt marsh conditions, though in historic times it also supported freshwater wetland or 'fen' along its river valleys. The whole zone is loosely referred to as the Outmarsh though this name refers strictly to the stretch between Humberston and Skegness; north of Grimsby the fringe of siltland along the Humber is known as the Humber Bank.

As in the Middle Marsh, modern arable farming has eroded but not completely removed the historic landscape of the Outmarsh, which

LEFT: **deserted church, Saltfleetby St. Peter**

FACING PAGE: **Skidbrooke church.** Skidbrooke was established as a daughter settlement of Cockerington some time before the Domesday Survey of 1086. The village was linked to the port of Saltfleet but became depopulated. St. Botolph's church survived in use until it too became redundant in the 1970s.

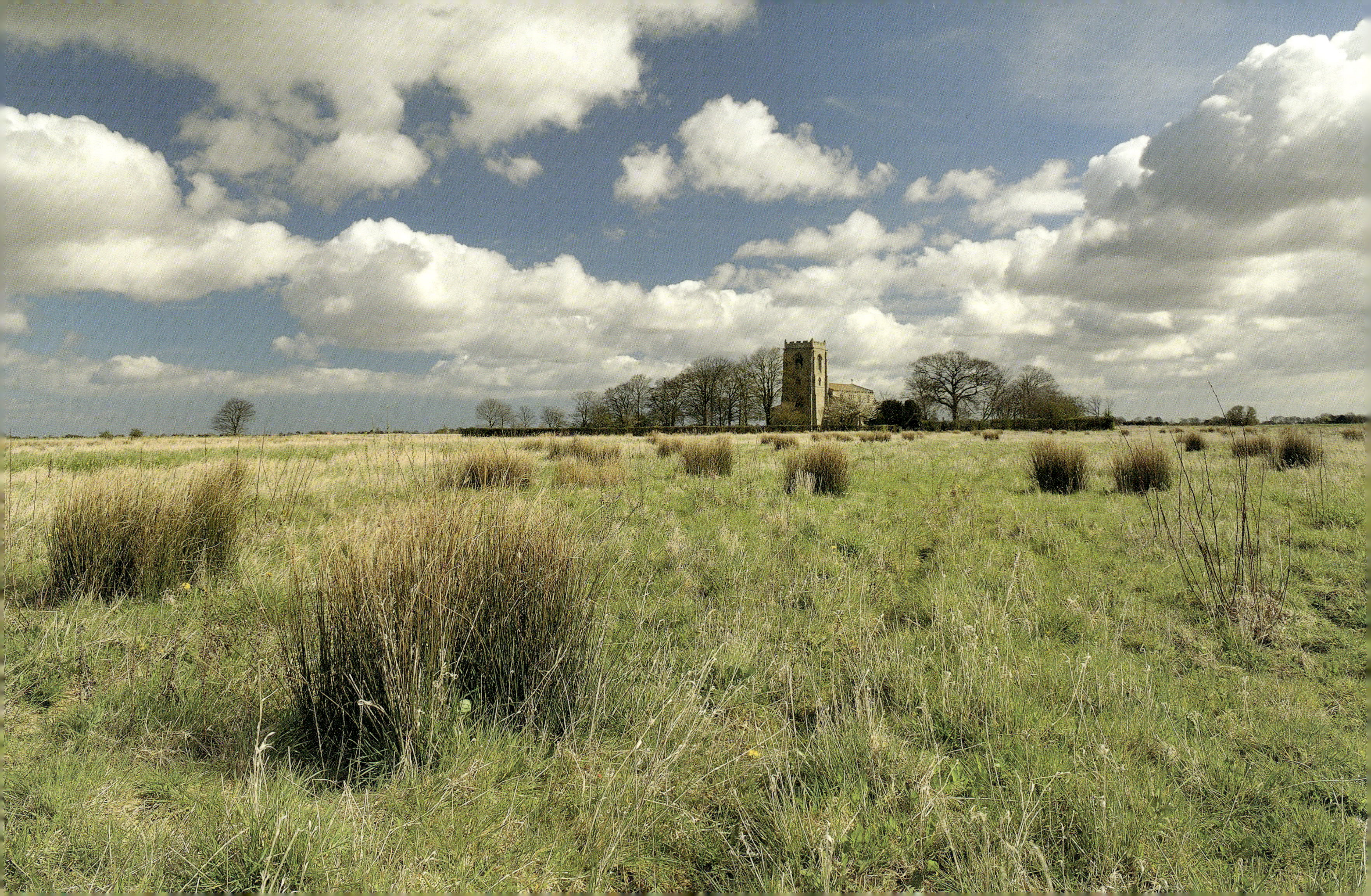

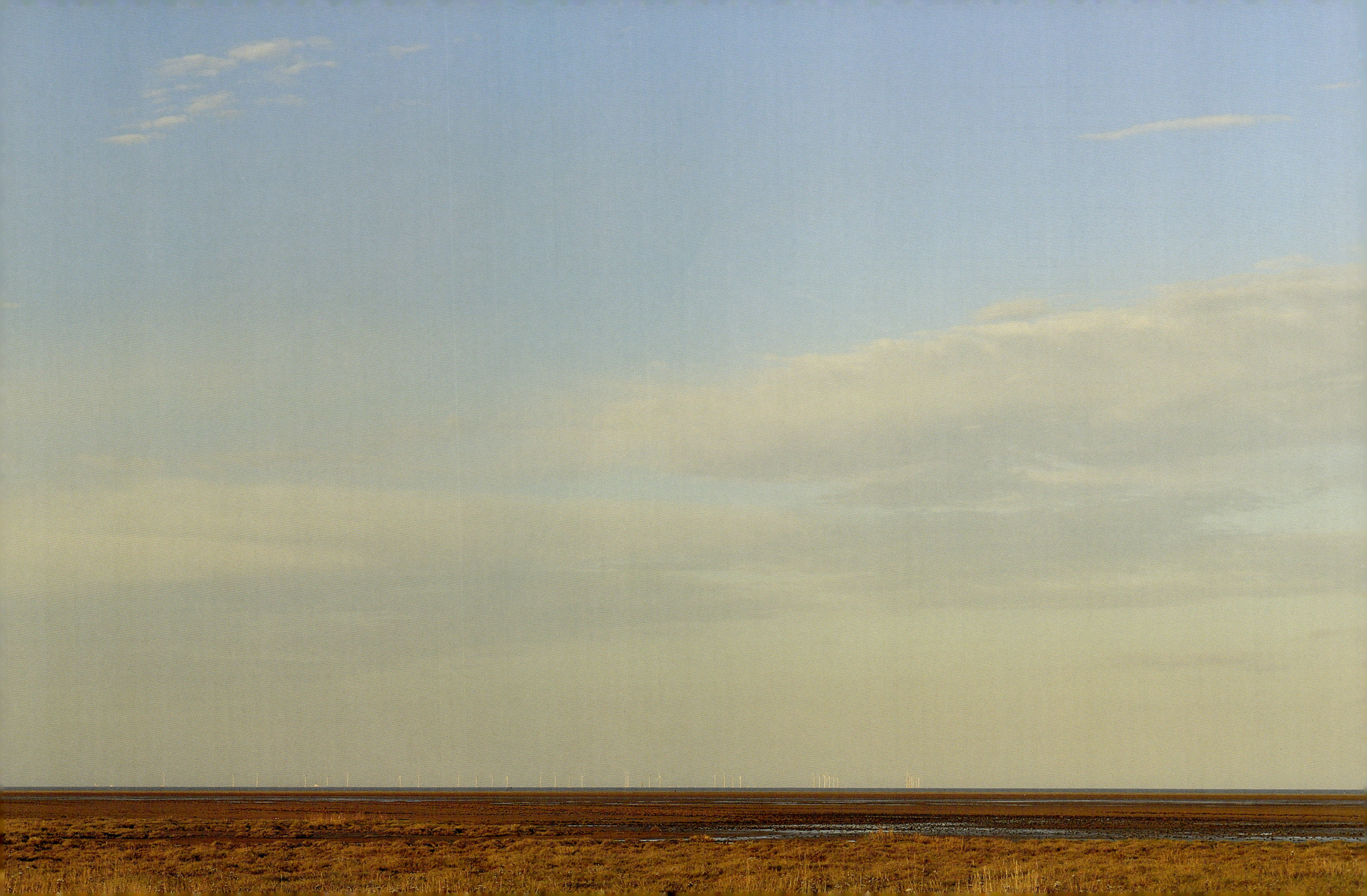

is here rooted in complex and varying patterns of Medieval colonisation and reclamation. It is thought that the area was mainly salt marsh in the Anglo-Scandinavian period, at which time it was used for grazing and salt production by the villages of the Middle Marsh. In the north of the Outmarsh, Medieval reclamation started not later than the 11th century as salter-graziers established seasonal 'cotes' along the high tide line. Evidence indicates that silt waste from salt making was used initially to raise the land surface to facilitate settlement and farming, these then being protected further by the construction of sea banks.

Over time the summer 'cotes' developed into more permanent daughter villages with their own field systems and churches. In some cases grand-daughter settlements were established and the earlier villages became depopulated as salt making moved seaward and then declined in the stormier climate of the late 13th and 14th centuries. Lost and shrunken villages are indicated by ruined or isolated churches as at Skidbrooke, Saltfleetby and Theddlethorpe. Further south the role of Medieval salt making is less clear, but new settlements such as Ingoldmells were established in the lee of coastal dunes. Here, protective sea banks were built to fill gaps in the dunes, including the so-called Roman Bank.

Reclamation of the Outmarsh wetlands was undertaken mainly in a piecemeal way without the need for more comprehensive drainage schemes or monastic involvement as seen in the Fens. Once coastal settlement and sea defences were established, the previously tidal marshland was brought into farming use and new 'ings' created by enclosure from the interior with its valley fens. This process also occurred outwards from the Middle Marsh

In contrast to the Wash coastline, with its reclaimed marshes, coastal erosion has prevented the growth of salt marsh and land reclamation along the southern portion of Lincolnshire's North Sea coast. Between Skegness and Mablethorpe land was actually lost to the sea from the late 1200s, including the original town of Skegness and five other Medieval churches. North of Mablethorpe, however, silt deposits from the Humber and the eroding Holderness coast have resulted in new land forming. Reclamation of salt marsh occurred between Saltfleet Haven and Humberston from the 17th century onwards using a succession of sea banks. Within the Humber estuary itself, silt deposition created a fringe of marshland that was reclaimed during the Parliamentary enclosures and also provided the raw material for the area's pantile and brick industry. Some salt marsh exists today beyond the Humber's man-made embankment but is now disappearing as sea level rises.

FACING PAGE: **salt marsh and mudflats near Donna Nook**

ABOVE: **former coastguard cottages, Tetney Lock**

The Lincolnshire coast is probably best known for its busy seaside resorts and caravan parks but it also retains large undeveloped stretches which are of high value for their natural landscape and wildlife. As well as beach and dune systems there are important areas of mudflats and salt marsh. Most of these wild areas are protected for nature conservation including the reserves at Donna Nook, Saltfleetby-Theddlethorpe Dunes and Gibraltar Point. Increasingly, the wildlife and archaeological value of the offshore landscape is also being recognised. It is hoped that the relict palaeo-landscape of sandbars, peat deposits and submerged forest off the present coastline will be designated as a Marine Conservation Area to protect its unique geology and wildlife from marine dredging and other threats.

LEFT: **sandbanks at low tide, Theddlethorpe St. Helen**

BELOW LEFT: **orchids in dune habitat, Rimac**

FACING PAGE: **dunes with marram grass and sea buckthorn, near Saltfleet.** Sea buckthorn (*Hippophae rhamnoides*) is widespread on the Lincolnshire coast, producing distinctive orange berries in the autumn.

and its till islands. Medieval field patterns consisting of blocks of elongated, ditched fields survive widely in the Outmarsh despite later changes, while ridge and furrow indicates that arable farming was important to the village economy in this period. Some seasonally-wet fenland remained until drainage improvements in the 19th century and is now being recreated along river valleys to benefit wildlife and flood management.

The eastern edge of the Outmarsh is defined by the coast itself which forms a distinct and dynamic zone where the sea and its tides are still the fundamental landscape influence. Most of it between Grimsby and

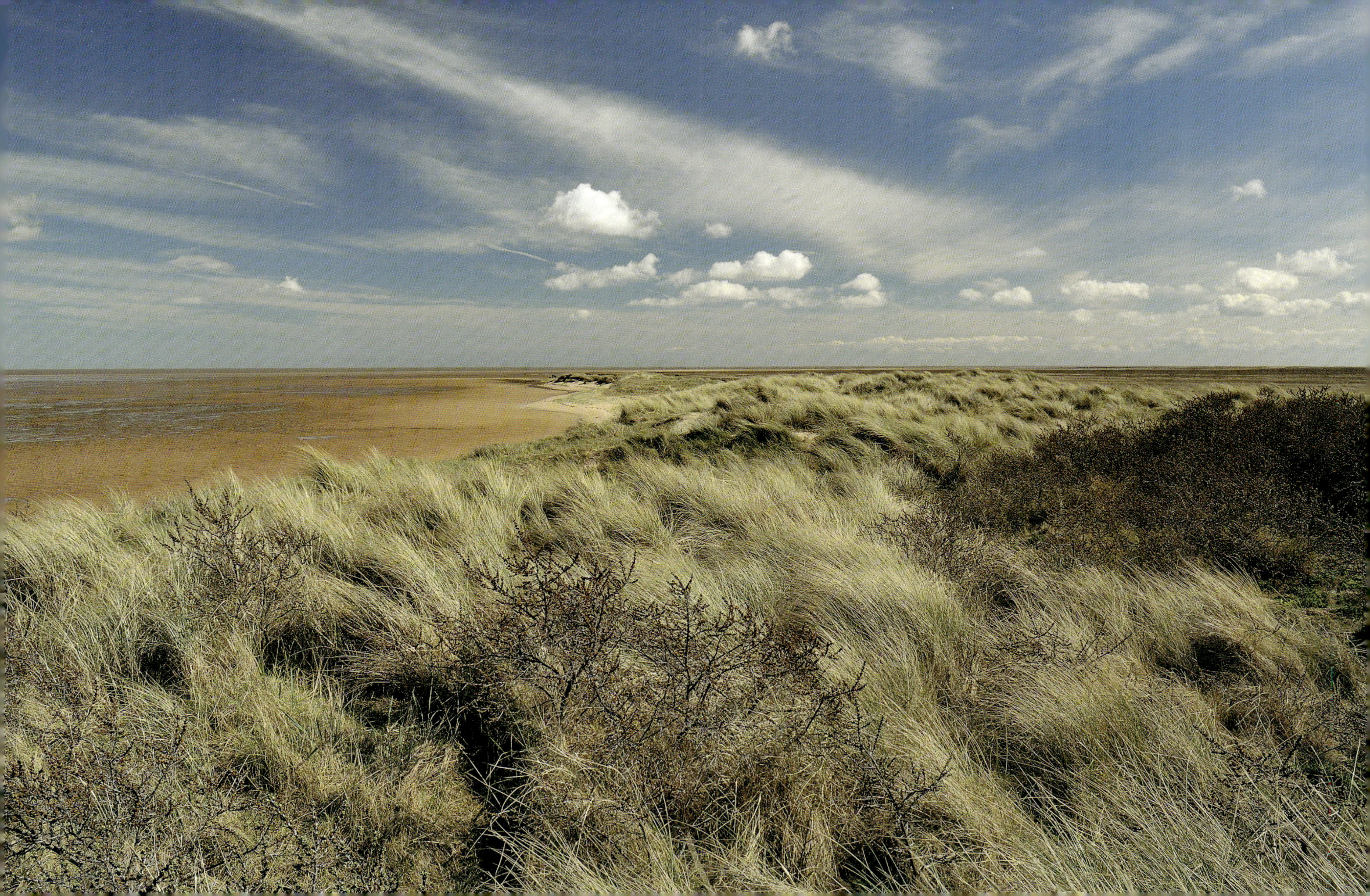

Gibraltar Point consists of a wide beach and foreshore of sand or mud that is backed by dune systems, some of which are several hundred years old. As befits Lincolnshire's gradual topography, sea cliffs are virtually absent, the only exceptions being at Cleethorpes and at South Ferriby Cliff in the Humber estuary. Overlying this natural pattern are human modifications, the most obvious being the development of coastal resorts and sea defences.

The rising sea level of our own, post-glacial epoch has placed much of Lincolnshire's coastline at risk of erosion and marine advance. Offshore islands and shoals of glacial sand and gravel provided a natural protective barrier for several millennia until they were breached and broken up by the storms of the late 13th century. Material from these was carried ashore where it formed storm beaches and dunes along much of the coastline. Since then, the balance between loss and gain of coastal land has varied with location depending on the amount of material left by the tide.

Between the Humber and Mablethorpe, deposition has historically offset the sea's rise and added new salt marsh and mudflats beyond the Medieval coastline. Similarly, Gibraltar Point is still growing outwards with material carried south along the coast. From Mablethorpe to Skegness, by contrast, the pattern is one of erosion and coastal retreat. Here, concrete 'seabees' now reinforce the dunes and, controversially, sand dredged offshore is used to 'nourish' the beaches. Global warming is expected to intensify coastal erosion and eventually reverse the land gains. Managed realignment is

LEFT: Haile Sands Fort from near Humberston Fitties

already underway in several locations to absorb the impact of storm surges and compensate for loss of salt marsh and other coastal habitats.

Early human use of the Marshland is difficult to assess overall due to the burial of prehistoric and Roman surfaces by later silts. The restricted archaeological record suggests that Neolithic settlement and agriculture were focused on the tills, from where the coastal marshes would have been exploited. Salt production had commenced by the Bronze Age and many saltern sites of Iron Age and Roman date have been identified beneath the surface of the Outmarsh. Roman roads or salt ways reached the coast in a number of places and a Roman shore fort is thought to have existed near present-day Skegness in connection with a ferry route across the Wash to Brancaster in north Norfolk. The process of early Medieval settlement on the Middle Marsh tills and subsequent expansion to reclaim and colonise the Outmarsh has been described already.

The coming of the railways saw small coastal villages with a few lodging houses for gentry visitors like the Tennyson family transformed into busy holiday resorts from the later 19th century onwards, including the re-establishment of a town at Skegness. By the 1920s, Lincolnshire's coastal dunes were experiencing heavy and unregulated use by car-borne visitors

TOP RIGHT: **seaside plot with dwelling, Humberston Fitties**

RIGHT: **promenade and beach huts, Chapel St. Leonards**

with caravans and tents as well as organised holiday camps and squatter camps of homeless families. Environmental and social concerns lead to landmark legislation in 1932 which enabled the local authorities to protect the Lincolnshire coast while also providing new housing. Humberston Fitties near Grimsby is a rare and interesting survival of unplanned, plot-based coastal development that originated as summerhouses for the better-off. Ironically, coastal protection was assisted by Government acquisition of land for bombing ranges at Theddlethorpe, Saltfleet and Donna Nook, though access in these areas remains restricted due to military activity.

Alongside the fine Medieval churches of the Outmarsh noted above, the Marshland boasts the tallest Medieval parish church spire in England – St.James' church in Louth is 295 ft (90m) tall – and the imposing brick and masonry gatehouse at Thornton Abbey dating from c.1380. As in Lincolnshire's other former wetlands, country houses are rare and most are located on the fringe of the Wolds like Gunby Hall. Traditional domestic and farm buildings are mainly of red brick and pantile with occasional survivals of mud and stud cottages in the villages.

The area has an important 20th century military heritage focused on the coastline and Humber, including the twin estuarial fortifications of Haile Sands Fort and Bull Sands Fort (Yorks).

ABOVE: **Thornton Abbey gatehouse**

FACING PAGE: **the Humber estuary at South Ferriby Cliff**

191

Further Reading

Barley, M.W. (1952)
Lincolnshire and the Fens
Batsford

Bennett, S. and N. (2001)
An Historical Atlas of Lincolnshire
Phillimore

Cousins, R. (2000)
Lincolnshire Buildings in the Mud and Stud Tradition
Heritage Lincolnshire

Cope-Faulkner et al (2010)
Wide Horizons: A History of South Holland's Landscape and People
Heritage Lincolnshire

Kime, W. (2005)
The Lincolnshire Seaside
Sutton Publishing

Osbourn, M. (2010)
Defending Lincolnshire: A Military History from the Conquest to the Cold War
The History Press

Robinson, D.N. (ed.) (2009)
The Lincolnshire Wolds
Windgather Press

Swinnerton, H.H. and Kent, P.E. (2nd edition, 1975)
The Geology of Lincolnshire
Lincolnshire Naturalists' Union

Thirsk, J. (1957)
English Peasant Farming: The Agrarian History of Lincolnshire from Tudor to Recent Times
Methuen

Thorold, H. and Yates, J. (1965)
Lincolnshire: A Shell Guide
Faber & Faber

Van de Noort, R. (2004)
The Humber Wetlands
Windgather Press

Wheeler, W.H. (1868)
A History of the Fens of South Lincolnshire
Cambridge University Press (2013)

Acknowledgements

Thanks to Anne Goldsmith, Martin Hayward Smith, Emma Osbourn, Brian Pattenden, Glyn Stocker, Adam Wilks, David Would and the Hooleys, plus the many others who helped me directly or indirectly in producing this book. Special thanks to Lois for her support throughout the book's lengthy evolution and for the many wonderful holidays and excursions together in Lincolnshire.